SLAVERY

Bondage Throughout History

SLAVERY
Bondage Throughout History

written and illustrated by Richard Watkins

Houghton Mifflin Company

Boston 2001

To my girls

www.houghtonmifflinbooks.com

The text of this book is set in 13.5-point Minion.
The illustrations are pencil and marker on vellum.

Library of Congress Cataloging-in-Publication Data

Watkins, Richard Ross.
Slavery : bondage throughout history / written and illustrated by Richard Watkins.
p.   cm.
ISBN 0-395-92289-5
1. Slavery—History—Juvenile literature. [1. Slavery—History.] I. Title.
HT861 .W37 2001   306.3'62'09—dc21   00-040752

Manufactured in the United States of America
LBM 10 9 8 7 6 5 4 3 2 1

CONTENTS

INTRODUCTION

Slavery has been a part of human civilization since the very beginning. Sumeria, the earliest culture to leave written records, practiced slavery 5,000 years ago. In the Sumerian records are inventories of items that were bought and sold. Someof these items were people, perhaps the earliest slaves. Every civilization since has enslaved its fellow human beings. Today, slavery is often thought of as a racial issue, which is hardly surprising, especially to African Americans. For them slavery is part of their recent heritage, full of painful memories of ancestors enslaved before the Civil War.

But slavery hasn't always been racially motivated. Throughout much of human history, race played no part whatsoever in slavery. In fact, more often than not, slave and master were of the same ethnic or cultural group. Sumerian enslaved Sumerian; Greek enslaved Greek; Christian enslaved Christian; black African enslaved black African. Every culture has been both slaver and enslaved. It is quite possible that each of us has not only an ancestor who felt the whip of slavery but also an ancestor who did the whipping.

Slavery is, unfortunately, part of our common human heritage and has been integral to the course of history. Human beings have always been one of the principal commodities of trade, and slaves built many of our great civilizations with their bare hands. The search for plentiful and inexpensive sources of slaves, as well as the quest for profitable markets for them, has sparked dramatic cultural shifts as wave after wave of people were forced to move throughout the world. The influx of slaves from all over Europe, Asia, the Middle East, and North Africa gave the Roman Empire its cosmopolitan flavor but also contributed to its eventual disintegration. The word *slave* comes from *Slav,* a name used to describe the millions of people from the Slavic regions of eastern Europe who were sold into slavery to the Muslims of southern Spain and North Africa during the Middle Ages. Merchants, made rich by the slave trade, financed the exploration of Africa and the New World that led to the destruction of the native cultures of the Americas. In their place was created a whole new culture.

The story is not over. Slavery still exists today, perhaps not on the grand scale of the past, but that hardly matters to those held in its chains.

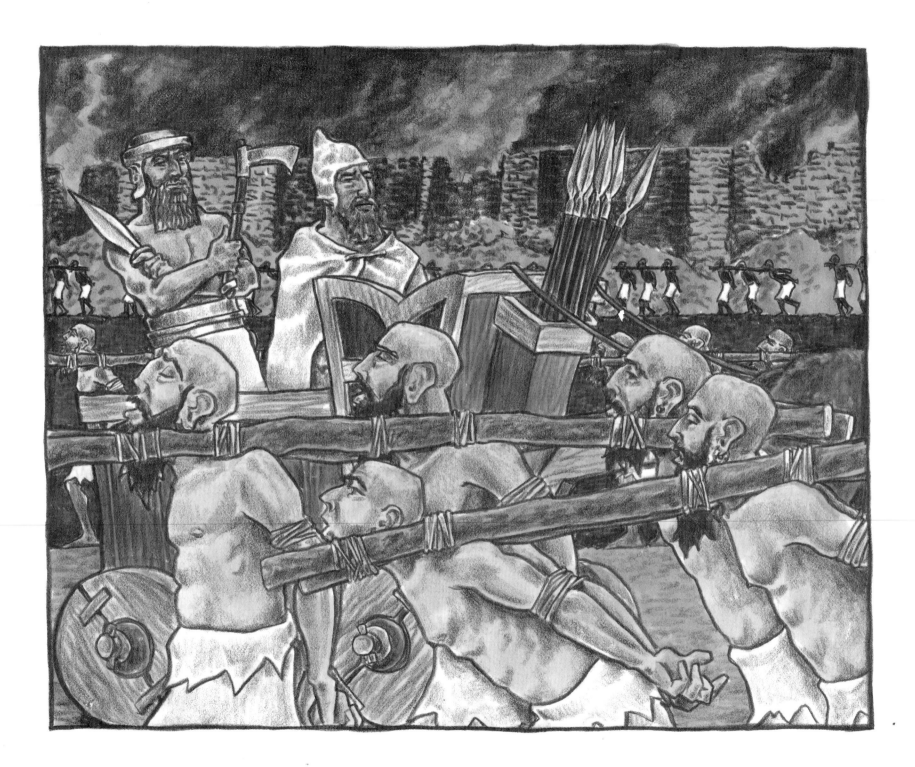

THE ANCIENT WORLD
& THE FIRST SLAVES

A slave is a person owned by another as a piece of property. Throughout history there have been many variations in the legal and cultural definitions of what a slave is but, simply put, a slave belonged to a master who could make the slave do anything he wanted. Slaves usually had no rights at all and no ability to make any decisions about their own lives. They ate what their masters gave them, they slept where they were told, and they worked until ordered to stop. If they didn't please their master, they could be sold, beaten, or even killed. Of course, there were exceptions—some slaves were treated well and lived their lives with a great deal of freedom. But the overwhelming majority suffered short and miserable lives.

The world's oldest civilizations were born in Mesopotamia, between the Tigris and Euphrates rivers (in what is now Iraq) around 4000 B.C. Small farming settlements gradually grew into cities when farming techniques improved enough for each settlement to increase its population and even produce surplus food that could be stored for future use. At this point it became apparent that whoever took possession of the land, even by force, could also possess the human beings

opposite: Sargon watches as captured enemy soldiers are driven into slavery.

Sargon, king of Sumeria.

who worked that land, gaining not only property but free labor. It then became practical to take captives after a battle, since feeding them would no longer be a strain on the food supply and the prisoners could be put to work or sold for profit. These early slaves were considered a valuable resource—human tools who could work the fields, tend the flocks, or labor in the mines.

Slaves also came to be thought of as status symbols, demonstrating the victor's power over his enemies. The rulers of early civilizations would proclaim their greatness and boast of the vast numbers of prisoners they had enslaved. Sargon, the most powerful king of Sumeria, the world's first great civilization, conquered every city in southern Mesopotamia in 2350 B.C. He owned 9,000 slaves. Rulers like Sargon also used slavery as a form of punishment for any of their own people who violated the law. Thieves were ordered to serve their victims as slaves, and the entire family of a convicted murderer could be enslaved to pay for the crime.

While Sargon and the priesthood were by far the biggest landholders and slaveowners, slaves were also found in most ordinary households, performing domestic chores—cooking meals, cleaning the house, or washing clothes. If their masters were farmers, slaves tilled the fields and tended the livestock; if their masters were merchants or tradesmen, slaves carried goods to market or worked in the shops. Sumerians faced with financial ruin often sold their children into slavery to pay off their debts. Boys worked as farmhands or craftsmen's assistants; girls worked as domestics, weavers, potters, bakers, or concubines. Orphans and illegitimate children were sent to live in the temples, growing up as slaves to the gods—maintaining the temples, or serving the priests.

Slavery was less important to Egyptian society than it was to other civilizations in the ancient world. The large population of peasant farmers who worked the rich soil of the Nile valley produced abundant food, so extensive slavery was unnecessary to support Egypt's agricultural needs, but many ancient Egyptians still owned slaves. Most slaves were captured in wars with neighboring tribes and cities.

It is often thought that Egypt's pyramids were built by slaves, but actually the pyramids and the other great construction projects of ancient Egypt were built by a huge labor force of as many as 100,000 peasant farmers who were ordered to the construction sites every year after their crops were harvested. These peasants were not considered slaves because they could not be bought or sold and could own their own homes, but their freedom was definitely limited. Most worked in fields owned by rich noblemen, the priesthood, or the pharaoh himself. The literal meaning of the word *pharaoh* is "great house," but in use it means "benevolent god." Technically, the pharaoh owned everything. Private ownership, be it of a business, land, or slaves, was only allowed with a blessing from the pharaoh. Most slaves were used as agricultural workers to produce the extra crops needed to feed the workers building the pyramids and other great construction projects. Others were drafted into the Egyptian military. Captured Sudanese, Libyans, and Syrians, as well as paid mercenaries, filled the ranks of the pharaoh's armies. The pharaoh occasionally rewarded military officers with a gift of slaves for exceptional service. One officer recorded the four slaves he received as a gift on the walls of his tomb.

The civilizations of Sumeria and Egypt, while unique in some respects, have much in common with every early culture. They all gave up their nomadic way of life when they learned to plant crops and domesticate animals. Their small settlements grew into villages and then cities. Governments were formed, gods were worshipped, great buildings and monuments were erected, and slaves were taken.

Sudanese mercenary of the Egyptian army.

SLAVE SOCIETIES

Even though slavery was universal there were some places where slavery was so important that societies couldn't survive without it. Ancient Greece, particularly Athens between the fifth and the third centuries B.C., was the first society to be dependent on slavery. Slaves did everything in ancient Greece: farming, cooking, cleaning; making tools, clothing, ships, and weapons; nursing babies; teaching students; performing in the theater; tending to the sick. There were only two occupations closed to slaves: politician and soldier. During its golden age, in the fifth century B.C., Athens had a population of approximately 155,000—60,000 free Greek citizens; 25,000 resident foreigners, called *metics;* and 70,000 slaves. The slave trade was big business. The majority of the slaves in Greece were bought through regular trade with non-Greek people around the Aegean Sea. Slave traders, generals, and pirates did business together to coordinate the supply of human cargo. They bargained over territories and haggled over prices. This seems a long way from the democratic ideals for which Greek civilization is so admired.

opposite: The Roman Forum. Everyone in this scene is a slave, a freed slave, or the descendant of a slave.

A slave sale in Rome.

In Rome, slavery was so common that there was virtually no part of Roman culture that did not have some relationship to, or dependence on, slaves. Slaves made up 30 percent of the population. By the end of the Roman Republic (29 B.C.), slaves performed all manual labor and were used in every craft and trade. Over the next two hundred years, the Roman army's wars of conquest flooded the empire with slaves. This glut of cheap labor forced low wages upon the dwindling number of free workmen, creating an underclass of poor freemen in the cities. Rome was by then completely dependent on slave labor.

During imperial times, the slave markets of Rome were the largest and busiest in the world, selling not only captured soldiers, but men, women, and children from every corner of the vast Roman Empire—miners from Dacia, teachers from Greece, stonemasons from Egypt, and house servants from Gaul.

Slaves owned by a small businessman or a minor government official would have to live on one bushel of grain each month, along with overripe olives, salted fish, and sour wine. Slaves typically were provided a new tunic every year, a heavy woolen cloak, and a pair of wooden clogs every two years. In the household of a rich Roman, the slaves were usually fed well and worked short hours, except for the senior household staff, who had to be on call twenty-four hours a day. This senior staff usually ate better than the rest of the slaves; their diet might include fish or poultry, maybe some cheese and better wine. The kitchen staff put in a lot of hours, but others, like the litter-bearers and the chambermaids, would have nothing to do all day if the master was away. These regular slaves dined on cakes made of barley or wheat, diluted wine, and occasionally some fruit.

In the Middle Ages, the rapid spread of Islam facilitated the creation of a slave society even larger than the Roman Empire's. From the middle of the seventh century until the end of the nineteenth century, some 18 million Africans were taken as slaves into Islamic countries. Add to this millions of enslaved Europeans, Slavs, and Asians and it's easy to see that slaves were as common in the early Islamic world as anywhere in history. It must be remembered that this Muslim world was actually made up of many countries and kingdoms, some lasting for decades, others for centuries, sometimes sharing no history or culture, only their faith in Islam. These huge numbers of slaves were necessary due in part to the commonly followed recommendation of Islamic law to free slaves after six years of bondage, so there was a continual need for new slaves.

Slavery was pervasive in Africa long before Arab and European traders arrived. Africans enslaved their fellow Africans throughout the continent. Powerful kingdoms were born in western Africa during the Middle Ages that practiced extensive slavery and later became instrumental in the international trade in human beings. In Ghana, one third of the population was enslaved between 1076 and 1600. The kingdom of Ghana was the major commercial center of trans-Saharan trade. Strategically positioned between the Sahara to the north and the gold fields to the south, Ghana became the most popular destination for traders from all over Africa. Here slaves were primarily used as domestic servants in wealthy households and as porters by merchants and traders to carry goods across the Sahara.

Mali was the greatest of the West African kingdoms. It was one of the largest empires in the world at its height and by far the richest kingdom in African history. Mali extended from the Senegal and Gambia rivers in present-day Ghana in the west, north to the great trading centers of Timbuktu and Gao, and almost to Lake Chad in the east in what is now Nigeria. Its prosperity was enhanced by its control over the trans-Saharan trade routes. It also possessed enormous natural resources: gold, copper, diamonds, and salt. Agricultural production was expanded largely because of the almost limitless supply of slave laborers. Large numbers of slaves were critical to support such a vast empire and were, along

Slave traders barter in Timbuktu.

with gold, Mali's most important export. Slaves were used in every area of society: in government, the military, industry, and agriculture. At least a third of the population was enslaved. Mali reached its peak during the reign of Mansa Musa, who took the throne in 1312. His brilliant leadership and diplomacy consolidated Mali's power over all of West Africa and ushered in a golden age of growth and prosperity. The great trading center at Timbuktu became the cultural center of Africa and the Islamic world. When Mansa Musa died in 1337, he left his kingdom one of the biggest, richest, and most famous empires in the world.

MANSA MUSA

When Mansa Musa made his pilgrimage to Mecca, as all devout Muslims must at some point during their lives, he made sure the whole world noticed his display of power and wealth as he traveled to the holy city. This was no ordinary, humble pilgrim. He brought one hundred camels loaded with gold pieces and eighty more that carried three hundred pounds of gold dust apiece. Five hundred slaves marched before him, each carrying a staff of solid gold. Another 12,000 slaves followed behind him, each dressed in the finest Persian silks and brocades. His favorite wife went with him and was attended by another five hundred slaves. He established diplomatic relations with the rulers of the lands he crossed and gave them extravagant gifts. He also gave alms to the poor he passed along the way. Once his pilgrimage was complete, he hired Abu Ishaq al-Sahili, a great architect and builder, to design a great mosque in Mali's capital city, Timbuktu. He also had the architect build a palace worthy of Mansa Musa's name.

Mansa Musa's pilgrimage did make him famous around the world, but historians now believe that he drained his kingdom's treasury to finance his ego-boosting journey.

Mansa Musa.

The Ashanti rose to power in the early eighteenth century along Africa's Gold Coast (the coastal region of modern Ghana). By forming a centralized government that united its people, the Ashanti virtually eliminated the capture and enslavement of any of its subjects by outsiders and successfully controlled all of the trade in the region. The Ashanti actively participated in the slave trade by capturing, buying, and selling great numbers of people from the surrounding areas. Some Ashanti slaves could own property (including other slaves), legally marry, testify in court, and inherit their master's property. Slaves were frequently adopted into the master's family, and succeeding generations became so intertwined that master and slave became indistinguishable.

Dahomey lies between modern-day Togo and Nigeria in West Africa. It was founded in the early seventeenth century by the Aja people. Dahomey was one of the most prominent participants in the Atlantic slave trade. One fifth of all the slaves sent to the Americas came from Dahomey or the areas around it. Most ended up working in the coffee, sugar, and tobacco plantations of Brazil.

In the nineteenth century, the Arab-Swahili culture of Zanzibar on the east coast of Africa was up to 90 percent slave. The trade in African slaves from the continent's eastern coast reached its peak in the 1800s, but it first developed into a large-scale international business in the eighth century. Arab merchants sailed down the African coast in *dhows* (Arabian sailing ships) full of grain, wine, fabrics, glassware, iron tools, and weapons. They traded for exotic animal furs and skins, ivory, and slaves. Over the centuries Arab traders settled among the local Africans. The mixture of Arab and African cultures gave rise to the Swahili people, with their own distinct customs and unique language. They became prosperous traders and were active in the slave trade that flourished in the eighteenth and nineteenth centuries. Slaves were taken from areas far inland, either by local tribes hired to hunt slaves or by the Swahilis themselves. Guns

A *dhow*, the ship most often used in the Arab world for the slave trade.

and ammunition were key barter items since they made the capture of large groups of slaves much easier. The Yao, Nyamwezi, and Kamba tribes were the most aggressive slave hunters in the region and dealt extensively with the Arab and Swahili traders on the coast. The brutality of the capture and transport of the slaves to the coast is hard to imagine. The demand for slaves was high, firearms were plentiful, and competition was fierce. These ingredients made for a dangerous business. A British missionary wrote that he had no doubt that four out of five captives died before they made it to the slave market.

At the same time that the great empires of Africa were flourishing, another empire was beginning its reign. The Ottoman Empire was founded in 1299 and grew to control all of the eastern Mediterranean. It lasted for over six hundred years and took millions of slaves from both the black African south and the white Slavic north. The percentage of its population that was enslaved was probably less than that of other slave cultures, but the influence of slavery was so pervasive in the Ottoman world that it has to be included among history's most slave-dependent societies. As in the Roman Empire, slaves were used in all occupations: domestics, artisans, merchants, and administrators; but unlike the situation in Rome, Ottoman slaves not only served in the military, they commanded it and controlled most of the government as well.

The Crimean Khanate (*khanate* means "kingdom," from the Mongolian word for king, *khan*) lasted from 1475 until 1783, and during its reign over the Crimean Peninsula in the Black Sea, it oversaw perhaps the most brutal slave state in history. The society depended on making regular raids on their Slavic and Caucasian neighbors and selling the captives in slave markets throughout the region. Three out of every four people were either slaves or freed slaves. Nearly every free man in the Crimea was involved in the slave business, either poor horsemen who got paid for catching slaves or the ruling elite who became rich selling them. It was a brutal business, even by slavery's cruel standards: for every

A Tartar slave hunter with his Caucasian captive.

10

slave sold, at least two or three more were killed during the raid and several more died before they reached the market.

A thousand miles to the west, in southern Europe, the slave trade was dominated by Italian merchants. From the thirteenth through the fifteenth century, while the rest of Europe evolved from slave societies to serf-supported societies, the slave trade still thrived in Italy. The aggressive trade practices of these merchants brought vast wealth to many Italian cities. How the slaves were captured was irrelevant as long as there was money to be made. One reason for the explosion of the Italian slave trade was the chronic labor shortage created by the Black Death, the wave of bubonic plague that swept across Europe beginning in 1348.

The streets of Florence, Genoa, and Venice, along with most other Italian cities, were flooded with slaves: Russians, Greeks, Moors (people of mixed North African and Arab descent), Ethiopians, and Tartars (Tartars are members of any of the Mongolian and Turkic tribes of eastern Europe and western and central Asia), people from all over Europe, Asia, and Africa. This was not the slavery of the past, where only the very rich kept slaves; everybody was a slaveowner. Of course, the rich kept huge estates full of slaves, but now tradesmen, artisans, and shopkeepers also had their own staffs of slaves. Most were used as domestic servants and shop assistants. The blacksmith had one to keep the forge hot; the baker's slave kneaded the dough and stoked the ovens. An industrious weaver would keep a few slaves busy at the looms upstairs while he sold the finished goods in the shop below. Even the most modest household had a slave to clean, cook, or fetch water. Large Italian cities in the fourteenth and fifteenth centuries were perhaps the most cosmopolitan cities in the world, but most of the people who created this international flavor—blond-haired Europeans, Tartars from central Asia, and dark-skinned Ethiopians—were not there voluntarily.

Slavery was commonplace in the New World, too. In Brazil, parts of the Caribbean, and the United States, slavery was as prevalent as it was in the world's

A wealthy Venetian lady and her slave girl.

Slaves harvesting sugar cane in Brazil.

other major slave cultures. Slavery became widespread in the Americas largely because of the development of large-scale sugar plantations. By the fifteenth century, sugar was one of Europe's most expensive luxury items. Sugar requires a great deal of human labor to cultivate, harvest, and process. The Portuguese were the first Europeans to realize that Africa was a huge source of human labor, and the other European powers quickly followed. Black slaves and sugar were introduced to the New World within ten years of Columbus's first voyage. The wealth generated by the increasing demand for sugar in Europe fueled the rapid growth of large-scale sugar cultivation in the Caribbean Islands, Mexico, and especially Brazil. All the European powers were competing for the resources of the New World and for the African slave labor to exploit them. By 1540, 10,000 Africans were sent by ship every year into slavery in the West Indies, Mexico, and South America. Nine hundred thousand Africans had been shipped to the Americas by 1600.

More slaves were sent to Brazil than anywhere else in the New World. They numbered more than four million. By 1800, slaves made up more than half of the population. Between 1790 and 1820, nearly a quarter of a million African slaves arrived in Cuban markets, and their labor turned Cuba into the world's largest producer of sugar. For seven straight years, beginning in 1833, a new ship with a fresh cargo of slaves entered Cuban ports every single week.

In the United States, tobacco was the first profitable crop that had required slave labor, then the invention of the cotton gin completely transformed the southern states' economy and the nature of American slavery. In 1790 there were 657,000 slaves in the South and 3,000 bales of cotton were produced. By 1860, there were nearly 4 million slaves who produced more than 4 million bales of cotton. In some states there were more slaves than free men. Sixty-four percent of South Carolina's people were slaves; 55 percent of Mississippi's.

SOLOMON NORTHUP

The daily routine of a slave on a cotton plantation in the southern United States was monotonous in its exhausting regularity. Solomon Northup, a free black man from the city of Washington who was kidnapped in 1841 and enslaved on a cotton plantation in Louisiana, wrote:

Solomon Northup.

"The hands are required to be in the cotton field as soon as it is light in the morning, and, with the exception of ten or fifteen minutes, which is given them at noon to swallow their allowance of cold bacon, they are not permitted to be a moment idle until it is too dark to see and when the moon is full, they often times labor till the middle of the night. They do not dare to stop even at dinner time, nor return to the quarters, however late it be, until the order to halt is given by the driver.

"Each one must then attend to his respective chores. One feeds the mules, another the swine—another cuts the wood, and so forth; besides, the packing is all done by candlelight. Finally, at a late hour, they reach their quarters, sleepy and overcome with the long day's toil. Then a fire must be kindled in the cabin, the corn ground in a small hand-mill, and supper, and dinner for the next day in the field, prepared."

Slaves living in the cities of the South experienced a very different life than those on the plantations. Masters found it profitable to hire out their slaves, so many of them enjoyed at least some degree of freedom, living apart from their masters and earning cash that bought better food and clothing. Some were leased for a specific job at a certain price and length of service. Others were lent out on a daily or even hourly basis. It came to be a common practice to allow slaves to find work for themselves. The slave then owed his master a fixed sum to be paid by the week, month, or sometimes year. Anything over that amount was the slave's to keep. Many city slaves were required to find their own places to live rather than return every night to their master's house. Those who continued to live under their master's roof usually stayed in rooms at the back of the house. In two-story homes, the slaves' rooms were above the kitchen or pantry. These rooms, however, usually had no beds; slaves had to sleep on the floor. The slaves who found their own living space used cellars, storage sheds, and attics. Living conditions were crude at best, but few would trade places with the field hands on the plantation.

Food was generally better for slaves in the city as well. Household servants usually ate out of the same kitchen as their masters, so even if they were limited to leftovers, they still fared better than rural slaves. If slaves were out on their own, they had to fend for themselves. There were general stores that sold only to black customers, and the white shopkeepers weren't supposed to sell to slaves without a master's permission, but since cash from a slave was as good as cash from a free man, the status of the customer was often ignored.

Many slaves in the cities of the South lived independent, but still very difficult, lives.

Many societies throughout history have had large slave populations; in fact, it is impossible to find any significant civilization that didn't use slaves or benefit from the slave trade. But the societies mentioned in this chapter would have developed very differently without slave labor. Some cultures may have not survived as long as they did, and a few, it can be argued, would never have existed at all without slavery.

BECOMING A SLAVE

The paths to slavery have been the same since the beginning of human history. The first and probably the most common way to become a slave was to be on the losing side of a war. If the defeated soldiers weren't slaughtered on the battlefield, they were sold off as slaves; the families of the losing army were almost always enslaved as well. The city-states of Sumeria were in a constant state of war with each other, which created a growing number of slaves. But since slaves often came from the nearest city and shared the same ethnic background as their captors, there was little social stigma attached to being a slave. Sometimes it was only temporary; slaves could buy back their freedom. War and slavery went hand in hand. Warfare not only provided a steady supply of slaves, it also created more demand. Citizens called to battle needed to find replacements to work in their fields and shops, and ships and weapons had to be made, so even more slaves were required in the shipyards, mines, and factories.

The Romans turned the production of slaves from prisoners of war into a major industry. The *quaestor*, or paymaster, of the conquering Roman general

opposite: Greek warriors lead a captured girl and her baby into slavery.

would organize a sale of the captured enemy soldiers to slave dealers who followed the army on their campaigns. Captured soldiers were sold in large groups for low prices to wholesale dealers right on the battlefield. Generals favored these quick sales because they generated instant cash to pay the troops and they freed the generals from the effort and expense of controlling large groups of prisoners. The dealers liked the bargain prices usually offered on the battlefields but were keenly aware of the financial risks involved. It could be quite expensive to transport large numbers of prisoners over long distances from battlefield to slave market. The dealers also knew that many of their purchases would die of exhaustion, disease, or suicide before they even got to market.

Being kidnapped by slave raiders or pirates was probably the second most

A roman general supervises a battlefield slave sale.

common path to slavery. Rare is the culture anywhere or at any time that didn't take advantage of a weaker neighbor. All of the early Mesopotamian cultures did it; so did the early Greeks and Romans. In Europe during the early Middle Ages, the Vikings were the most aggressive slave raiders, but other Europeans hunted for slaves, too, even after they gave up their pagan gods and converted to Christianity. They didn't just catch other Christians, either. Arabs, Africans, and North American Indians took every opportunity to snatch their neighbors, use them as slaves, or sell them to another group who did.

Viking raiders row out to sea with a cargo of new slaves.

Greeks could find themselves abducted by pirates who roamed the coastline raiding farms and villages for loot and slaves. Actually, these pirates were also legitimate traders when it was profitable enough, but they could never resist an easy target. The Aegean and Mediterranean seas were crowded with ships that engaged in legitimate trade one day and piracy or kidnapping the next. Indian tribes of America's Pacific Northwest organized raiding parties that often traveled hundreds of miles searching for victims. This made revenge more difficult and discouraged escape attempts. In the early Middle Ages, the Vikings used northern and eastern Europe as their human hunting grounds. In some places they would leave their quarry unmolested until they needed to restock for their next trading expedition, then they would simply round up the number of villagers they needed and ship them off to the slave market. In Kiev, Russia, local chieftains were forced to have their own people vote on who among them would be given over to the Vikings to be sold.

Enslavement as punishment for a crime was widespread among the ancient Middle Eastern civilizations of Sumeria, Assyria, and Babylon. African tribes also enslaved criminals, and this practice became even more widespread in the sixteenth century, to meet the demands of the transatlantic slave trade. The Ashanti and the Dahomeans condemned most of their criminals to slavery and then sold them to European traders. As recently as the twentieth century, the Soviet Union sentenced millions of people convicted of crimes to forced labor camps, a form of enslavement. Only a tiny percentage of those convicted were actually guilty of committing crimes. The vast majority were convicted of offenses against the state: speaking out against the government, attending banned religious services, or associating with anyone considered disloyal to the Communist Party.

Poverty and debt forced millions into slavery. Selling oneself or a family member to pay off a debt has been documented in every society that practiced slavery. Sumerians who were enslaved to pay off a debt were freed after a set length of time. A father could give one of his children or his wife to his creditor to settle his debt, but by law such slavery was limited to a term of three years. There were some variations; for example, family members of Aztec debt slaves were allowed to take turns working as the slave, if the owner agreed. Debt slavery was common for much of China's long history, especially in times of famine. During the Ming Dynasty (1368–1644), debt slaves were called *bugu* and were considered to be of slightly higher status than regular slaves. *Bugu* received payment for their food and clothing and could not be sold by their masters though they could be given away. Struggling English families in the Middle Ages sometimes had no choice but to sell a child into slavery and use the money to keep the rest of the family alive. A record survives from a certain Archbishop Wulfstan, who wrote in 1014, "Also we know full well where that miserable deed has occurred that a father has sold his son at a price, or a son his mother, or one brother another, into the power of foreigners."

The final and perhaps the most unlucky way to become a slave was to be born a slave. In many cultures, if your parents were slaves, so were you. You didn't have to be a slave forever though, at least in some places. A Sumerian slave could earn enough money to buy his freedom, and so could some Roman slaves. But elsewhere, if you were born a slave, you died a slave. In parts of China, for instance, whole families would be enslaved to other families for generation after generation.

A debt slave, or *bugu,* of China's Ming Dynasty.

REASONS FOR SLAVERY

In many cases slavery grew out of an "us" versus "them" mentality. "Us" looked like us, talked like us, and lived like us. Therefore "us" were equal and deserved certain basic rights. "Them" was anyone different. Sometimes it was only a tiny difference—a different tribe, a different village or city. People looked at a neighboring kingdom or nation as different. Until very recently, different meant inferior, not as good or as smart or as strong, and therefore not worthy of respect or even any basic rights. With these attitudes it was always easy to make "them" slaves. The idea that everyone is equal and entitled to basic human rights is a modern one and still not recognized in some parts of the world.

Perhaps the most enduring legacy of ancient Greece was the invention of democratic government. The election of government by free citizens, each with equal rights, was a landmark of social progress. This breakthrough, however, did not interfere in any way with the institution of slavery. Even the most enlightened Greek citizen believed that slavery was not only natural but necessary. The philosopher Aristotle wrote, "These people are slaves by nature, and it is better for them to be subject to this kind of control. For a man who is able to belong to

opposite: Greek nobility relax as their slaves go about their chores.

another person is by nature a slave." Nowhere in Greek literature does there appear any consideration of a slave as a complete human being, equal in any way to his master. Free Greeks in the fifth century B.C. took their superiority over slaves for granted; slaves were only tools. They were usually treated humanely, though not for humanitarian reasons. It was prudent to treat slaves well because an abused slave was usually less productive than a content one. It also reflected poorly on a Greek citizen if he had to resort to brutality to keep his slaves in line.

The early Christian Church justified the institution of slavery just as the Romans had; it stated that some people were meant to be masters and others were meant to be slaves. St. Augustine wrote in his book *The City of God,* "The justice of masters dominating slaves is clear, because those who excel in reason should excel in power." The Church made no efforts to eliminate slavery and was itself a major slaveowner.

Slavery was taken for granted in Islam just as it was in Judaism and early Christianity. The Prophet Muhammad owned slaves, as did his inner circle of followers. A basic principle of Islam is that one human being has the right to control the life of another. The Koran says that the inequality between master and slave was ordained by God. It was forbidden under Islamic law, however, to enslave any free Muslim or any Christian or Jew living under Muslim rule.

When Columbus reached the New World in 1492, he was the first of many to exploit the widely held belief that Christian Europeans had the right—even the duty—to conquer and enslave the indigenous people they found. He wrote, "From here, in the name of the Blessed Trinity, we can send all the slaves that can be sold." Columbus found the Indians on the island he called San Salvador in the Bahamas to be "extraordinarily timid . . . but once their fear has left them, they give proof of an innocence and a generosity that can scarcely be believed. No matter what is asked of them, they never refuse it, and show themselves contented with any gift offered them. . . . They are people of noble bearing."

Christopher Columbus.

Capturing them was not a problem because "these people are very unskilled in arms. . . . With fifty men they could all be subjected and be made to do all that I wished." Columbus put five hundred Taino Indians from Española (present-day Hispaniola, which is divided between Haiti and the Dominican Republic) aboard four caravels bound for Spain. Two hundred died on the way. The survivors were sold in the slave market in Seville, but they were so weakened by their ordeal that they died soon after. There were an estimated 3 million Taino Indians on Española when Columbus arrived; by 1515, diseases unknowingly brought by the Spanish, brutal slave labor, and simple murder had wiped out all but 1,500 of them.

Through much of history, justification for slavery was unspoken and unnecessary. It was just a normal part of everyday life. Masters couldn't imagine life without slaves out in the fields or in the kitchen, and slaves, for the most part, couldn't imagine life as free men or women. Many were slaves their whole lives, as their parents and grandparents had been, and expected that their children would be slaves, too. On the rare occasions when a slaveowner sympathized with the plight of his slaves and struggled with his conscience over the morality of slavery, he usually felt forced by economic necessity to overlook humanitarian concerns. Releasing slaves could spell economic ruin for a Roman nobleman or Southern U.S. plantation owner, regardless of his good intentions. For those in the slave business, slavery had nothing to do with cultural or racial superiority; it was strictly a matter of money. The opportunity to make a large profit overwhelmed any consideration slave traders might have had for the people whom they bought and sold like cattle.

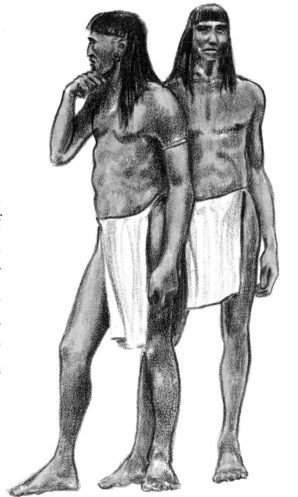

The Taino Indians would regret meeting Columbus.

TRADE ROUTES FOR SLAVES IN AFRICA

The routes taken by slave caravans all across Africa were well worn by centuries of use. They radiated out from the interior of the continent toward the coast: north through the Sahara to trade centers on the Mediterranean; east to the Indian Ocean, where Swahili traders packed their human cargo aboard *dhows* bound for the major ports of the Middle East; and west to the Atlantic Ocean, where millions faced a nightmarish voyage that ended in either death or a life of slavery in the New World.

Historically, Africa has had the misfortune of being the source of tens of millions of slaves. Africa was targeted as the best place to obtain slaves in the two periods of history (after the Roman Empire) that demanded the greatest numbers of slaves: the rise of Islam and the European conquest of the New World.

Muslim and European slave traders did not simply march into Africa, abduct native people out of their villages, and send them off into slavery. It was usually Africans who did the abducting. Europeans didn't try to invade the kingdoms; they used Arab middlemen to work their way into the African slave trade. These Arab merchants and the black tribal rulers had a trading network that was

opposite: A slave caravan crosses the Sahara Desert.

centuries old. They used diplomacy and careful trade negotiations to establish a foothold in Africa. When the Portuguese and later other Europeans landed on the western coast of Africa, they built their trading posts and fortresses with the blessing of the local leaders, who received substantial rent payments from their European tenants.

The effect of the explosive growth of Islam, which began in the seventh century, on the slave trade in Europe was equaled, if not surpassed, by a trade in slaves from central Africa north across the Sahara Desert and into the Muslim world. For nearly a thousand years, people were captured from sub-Saharan Africa and marched by caravan to North Africa. From there they were sold as slaves to local buyers or shipped abroad to markets across the Mediterranean. Without the camel, regular trade across the Sahara would have been impossible. Traders had crossed the desert on horses and ox carts since 1000 B.C., but after camels were domesticated in the fourth century, their ability to carry heavy loads in extreme conditions made them ideal desert pack animals, and trade across the desert blossomed.

There were three major routes through the Sahara Desert: from Timbuktu (in Mali) to Morocco; from Kano (near Lake Chad) to Fezzan (in Libya); and from Darfur (in western Sudan) to Egypt. The merchants who made the journey were mostly Muslim, but there were Berber (non-Arab, North African tribesmen), blacks, and Jewish traders, too. The eastern route into Egypt was called the Forty Days Road, while the western route from Timbuktu took between seventy and ninety days, if all went well. Sandstorms, drastic temperature changes, even an occasional blizzard could spell disaster. Bandits were a constant threat and water was as scarce as it was necessary. The journey across the desert was every bit as dangerous as an ocean crossing. The financial rewards had to justify such a difficult trip—after all, the merchants were after profits, not adventure. That

There were three major routes across the Sahara Desert. *From left to right:* Timbuktu to Morocco; Kano to Fezzan; Darfur to Egypt.

meant that the goods carried across the desert had to be very valuable relative to their weight. Grain, for example, was much too bulky; the price of grain did not warrant risking one's life to transport it across the Sahara. It was the expensive and the exotic items that were sought: rare spices, fragrances such as frankincense, and, of course, gold and ivory. Slaves were the most important commodity of all because they generated high profits and they transported themselves. They could also carry merchandise on their backs or balanced on their heads—a bonus for traders.

At first, slaves were traded for salt, which was a scarce and therefore valuable commodity in central Africa. Later, horses and guns were bartered for slaves. In the late eighteenth and early nineteenth centuries, cowrie shells from the Indian Ocean were the most important item traded for slaves. Cowrie shells were used as currency in some parts of Africa.

The experienced slave caravan leader knew how to avoid the heat of the Sahara summer and the equally dangerous winter cold. The caravans followed a yearly schedule to cross the Sahara in the best weather. They left North Africa in September or October for Sudan, where the caravans spent the winter. They began their return trip in April or May.

Even after the Europeans established trade relationships with the kingdoms of western Africa and began exporting large numbers of slaves across the Atlantic, the trade across the Sahara continued to thrive. In the 1700s, caravans carrying nothing but slaves were commonplace in the trading centers of North Africa. Even in the 1800s, when slavery was beginning to decline, there were African kingdoms completely dependent on the export of slaves for income. It is difficult to estimate the numbers of black Africans taken into slavery along the trans-Saharan caravan routes. Some historians assert that more than 15 million slaves were sold in North Africa and the Middle East in the trade that continued until the end of the nineteenth century, but there is no way to know how many others died along the way, forever buried beneath the sands of the Sahara.

After the European powers conquered the Americas and nearly wiped out the native populations, they looked to Africa to provide the labor to allow them to fully exploit the vast resources of the New World. It didn't take long to develop an efficient system to move great numbers of Africans across the Atlantic. The transatlantic slave trade would grow to become one of the biggest business ventures in history. It was also one of the world's largest forced migrations. Approximately 11 million black slaves were shipped from Africa to the Americas between 1492 and 1870, and at least 1 million died along the way. The Portuguese were the first to take Africans to the New World and enslaved more people than any other nation. Following, in order of scale, were the English, French, Spanish, Dutch, and Americans. African kings and traders had close business relationships with the Europeans, and many made fortunes trading their countrymen as slaves for guns, alcohol, horses, and cloth.

HENRY THE NAVIGATOR

In 1441 a small Portuguese caravel commanded by Antao Goncalves sailed down the Atlantic coast of Africa. He led his crew ashore on a raiding party. They didn't find much worth plundering, but they did capture twelve of the local people and took them aboard the ship. Upon Goncalves's return to Lisbon, he presented his African prisoners as gifts to Prince Henry, brother to the king of Portugal and known as the Navigator because of his interest in seafaring and exploration. Prince Henry immediately recognized the potential of the twelve unfortunate men. Ever the good Catholic, he wrote to the pope seeking approval for more expeditions to capture

Henry the Navigator.

more people to use as slaves. The pope replied by granting Portugal the right to enslave any heathens, or non-Christians.

Henry's court became the European center for mapmaking, shipbuilding and navigational research. All this knowledge was used to further Portuguese exploration and trading opportunities. At the end of the fifteenth century, Vasco da Gama led three ships around Africa to India; Portuguese traders penetrated deep into Asia via the rivers and inland seas of eastern Europe; and the Atlantic coast of South America and the Amazon River were first explored by Portuguese seafarers. Henry was responsible for the rapid Portuguese expansion that took place over the next century, which, in turn, sparked the transatlantic slave trade.

Intertribal warfare provided many fresh captives to the European traders waiting in their fortresses along the coast. Slavery came to change the nature of warfare in West Africa. Until the late fifteenth century, wars in Africa were relatively small in scale. Intertribal conflicts were about settling grievances or saving face. The demand for slaves created war for profit. Attacks were made for the sole purpose of taking prisoners, and success was measured by how many people were captured.

Roughly three-quarters of the slaves taken to the New World came from the area of West Africa north of the Congo River, occupied today by Dahomey, Ghana, and Nigeria. Captives were taken in raids and wars inland, marched to the coast, and sold to African middlemen who then traded them to the Europeans. To avoid enslavement themselves, people always looked to the next group inland as a source of slaves. As long as slaves kept coming out of the interior, those closer to the coast wouldn't become targets of the slave hunters.

Young men were the finest catch for the slavers because the plantations wanted-ed strong field workers who could be put to work immediately, but they took much more effort to capture and could put up a fight. Women and children were easier targets but were not worth as much at the markets and were often kept in Africa as domestic slaves. The old and the infirm were killed on the spot, not worth the trouble.

Millions upon millions of slaves were marched along the slave trade's well-traveled routes in Africa. Most would end up far from home, and few would ever return. Taken in its entirety, the African slave trade probably moved more people than any other forced migration in history.

Slave hunters raid an African village.

Portrait of a slave hunter.

BUYING A SLAVE

Slaves could be bought and sold like any product or service, but most often they were auctioned off to the highest bidder. In the earliest times, any open area or public square would suffice for a slave auction; the marketplace in every village or city was the most logical place to find slaves for sale. As the trade in people became a more specialized business, with buyers and sellers dealing almost exclusively in slaves, special markets and warehouses were used to hold and sell the human inventory.

Greek slaves were sold in the *agora,* the city's business center. They stood in front of the buyers who inspected them closely before they bid, prodding them with staffs, forcing open their mouths to check their teeth, and holding up words written on placards to see if they could read, which increased their value considerably.

Roman slaves were usually sold at public auction. Those who were up for sale had their feet covered in white chalk and a scroll tied around their necks. This scroll listed the slave's name, country of origin (if foreign born), special skills or training, and a statement of health. There was usually a six-month, money-back

opposite: Potential buyers inspect a slave girl in a Roman slave market.

guarantee. If the slave couldn't do what was claimed on the scroll or if he was sickly or a thief, he could be returned for a refund. As slaves came up for sale, they mounted a platform and the auctioneer described their qualities. Potential buyers were invited to inspect them, check teeth, evaluate muscle tone, and judge physical attractiveness. Those put on the block wearing a woolen cap were judged to be of low quality or defective in some way and were sold with no guarantee—as is, no refund, all sales final. Exceptionally beautiful slaves, either male or female, or those with extraordinary skills or talents were often sold at private, invitation-only auctions.

A slave auction in Kaffa.

In the fourteenth and fifteenth centuries, the Italians established trading centers on the coast of the Black Sea to expedite trade with eastern Europe and Asia. The largest, Kaffa (now called Feodosiya, Russia), was run by the Genoese. A Spaniard named Pero Tafur wrote that in Kaffa's slave market "They sell more slaves both male and female than anywhere else in the world. . . . The selling takes place as follows. The sellers make the slave strip to the skin, males as well as females, and they put on them a cloak of felt, and the price is named. Afterward they throw off their coverings, and make them walk up and down to show whether they have any bodily defect. If there is a Tartar man or woman among them, the price is a third more, since it may be taken as a certainty that no Tartar ever betrayed a master."

During the height of the transatlantic slave trade there was such a demand for workers on the rapidly expanding plantations and mines of the New World that slaves would sometimes be bought in large groups straight off the ships. One selling method, the scramble, had to be terrifying for slaves just forced off a ship into a strange new land. First the injured, sick, and dying were marched or carried to a local tavern and sold for as little as a dollar apiece. The healthy ones were then paraded through town, led by musicians who announced their arrival.

Potential buyers and curious onlookers met them at the public square for closer inspection. The scramble was a wild free-for-all. Buyers literally scrambled to grab hold of the slaves they wanted. Slaves were driven into a pen surrounded by a mob of screaming buyers, pushing and shoving to get a good position. When the starting gun was fired, the gate was thrown open and the buyers swarmed into the pen to grab the finest specimens. Buyers punched and kicked each other and yanked slaves out of each other's grip. The most aggressive, determined buyers carried ropes and used them to encircle as many slaves as possible. Faced with this chaos the slaves sometimes panicked, bolted from the holding pen, and raced through the streets while the mob gave chase. After they were paid for, slaves were branded with the mark of their new owners, usually on the chest or shoulder.

A slave scramble.

In the southern United States before the Civil War, the buying and selling of slaves was a part of everyday life. Slaves had to face the prospect of being sold off at the whim of their masters. Slaves who were up for sale were taken to a trading center in town. Every town had a slave pen, which could be an empty stable, a room built onto the back of a store, or a warehouse devoted solely to the slave trade. After Solomon Northup was freed, he wrote his story, *Twelve Years a Slave*. Within two years of its publication, 27,000 copies had been sold. His book provides a comprehensive view of the life of the plantation slave. Northup, who was held in several slave pens, described the procedure at the slave house of Theophilus Freeman in New Orleans.

A SLAVE SALE

"In the first place we are required to wash thoroughly, and those with beards, to shave. We were then furnished with a new suit each, cheap, but clean. The men had hat, coat, shirt, pants, and shoes; the women frocks of calico, and handkerchiefs to bind about their heads. We were now conducted into a large room in the front part of the building to which the yard was attached, in order to be properly trained, before

the admission of customers. Freeman charged us to remember our places; exhorted us to appear smart and lively—sometimes threatening, and again, holding out various inducements. During the day he exercised us in the art of 'looking smart,' and of moving to our places with exact precision.

"After being fed, in the afternoon, we were again paraded and made to dance. Bob, a colored boy who had some time belonged to Freeman, played on the violin. . . .

"Next day many customers called to examine Freeman's 'new lot.' The latter gentleman was very loquacious, dwelling at much length upon our several good points and qualities. He would make us hold up our heads, walk briskly back and forth, while customers would feel of our hands and arms and bodies, turn us about, ask us what we could do, make us open our mouths and show our teeth, precisely as a jockey examines a horse which he is about to barter for or purchase. Sometimes a man or woman was taken back to the small house in the yard, stripped, and inspected more minutely. Scars upon a slave's back were considered evidence of a rebellious or unruly spirit, and hurt his sale."

The separation of loved ones was a very real threat to slaves in the American South. Some masters kept families together, but most thought nothing of ripping them apart. This ad, placed by one J. T. Underwood on May 2, 1849, in the Louisville *Weekly Journal*, gives us a hint of the casual attitude taken in the sale of slave families: "I wish to sell a Negro woman and four children. The woman is 22 years old, of good character, a good cook and washer. The children are very likely from 6 years down to 1½. I will sell them together or separately to suit purchaser." There were pages of ads similar to this in every newspaper, exactly like the want ads in today's newspapers, except that the ads of the Old South offered people for sale, not used cars.

Slaves usually did not come cheap. In Sumeria during the Akkad dynasty (2350–2230 B.C.), a slave cost between ten and fifteen shekels of silver. By com-

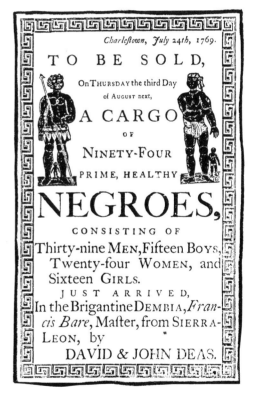

A newspaper advertisement for a slave sale.

parison, a bushel of barley was worth one shekel, as was a sheep. A bull might cost as much as a female slave, 10 shekels. Slaves were very expensive in ancient Egypt as well. During the eighteenth dynasty (1550–1295 B.C.) a female slave cost four *deben* of silver, a male slave seven *deben*. Twelve *shat* equaled one *deben*. Prices for other trade items demonstrate the high cost of slaves: A goat only cost half a *shat,* a cow eight *shat,* and a house ten *shat.* According to these values, a male slave cost more than eight times as much as an average Egyptian's house.

Prices in ancient Greece varied according to the age, sex, and skill of the slave. Children were less expensive because of the time and effort required to train them for a particular purpose. Owners were reluctant to spend much on a young slave who might or might not produce a profit. Archaeologists have found a document that lists the prices paid for slaves in Syria (which was a colony of Greece) around A.D. 260 at twenty drachmas for a small boy. A strong but unskilled man brought much more; he might end up working in the fields or in a silver mine, someplace where a strong back and a weak mind were useful. The Greek writer Xenophon estimated that the average price of the slaves working in the silver mines of Laurium was 180 drachmas. The most expensive slaves, however, were those with exceptional skills—accountants, business managers, teachers, and doctors, for example. One Greek aristocrat paid 6,000 drachmas for a slave who could manage his silver mine. To get an idea of what a slave was worth, compare these prices from ancient Greece: A skilled construction worker at one of Athens's public buildings earned just two drachmas a day, and a decent mule cost around two hundred drachmas.

Considering the Roman Empire's dependence on slaves at every level of its society, it's not surprising that the prices paid for them varied widely. A slave of average quality with no special skills went for between 500 and 600 *denarii.* Skilled slaves such as artists and craftsmen cost over 2,000 *denarii,* and slaves with an education cost at least 8,000 *denarii.* Of course there was no limit to what wealthy Romans would spend on slaves who were especially beautiful or talented. The Roman historian Suetonius wrote that an aristocrat once paid 175,000 *denarii* for a brilliant teacher, only to set him free. By comparison, a Roman soldier earned 225 *denarii* each year, and that was at least twice what a free Roman laborer made. A small apartment in one of the thousands of cramped apartment blocks in Rome rented for 500 *denarii* a year.

Slaves traded by the Pacific Northwest Indian tribes were worth a specified amount of dentalia, or tooth shells. These seashells were the form of currency used by all the Native American tribes along America's Pacific coast. How many strings of shells a slave was worth depended not only on the skills he or she offered a potential buyer, but also where the slave was being sold. Since the shells were found mostly on the west coast of Vancouver Island, a slave sold there would earn many more shells than one sold elsewhere. For example, records indicate that a slave on Vancouver Island cost five strings of dentalia, each string measuring the length from fingertip to fingertip of outstretched arms. In northern California, where dentalia were rare, a slave could be bought for just one string of shells.

From the beginning of the transatlantic slave trade, European traders found that their African suppliers wanted only European goods and luxury items in return for slaves. Africans wanted horses, cookware, china, tools, and silk and other fabrics. In 1455 a Portuguese trader could get 18 slaves for one horse. As the trade grew, the African suppliers became more demanding. In 1740 an English slave ship traded the following items for 180 slaves: 1,170 silver coins, 430 iron bars, 92 cutlasses, 430 gun flints, 1,162 kilograms of salt, 30 kilograms of linen, 130 kilograms of Manchester cloth, 108 kilograms of Indian textiles, 219 kilograms of woolen cloth, 47 reams of paper, 164 guns, 71 pairs of pistols, 518 kilograms of gunpowder, 16 kilograms of lead balls, 102 brass pans, 301 kilograms of pewterware, 2 rods of copper, and 119 gallons of rum. Included also were an assortment of beads and shells, which were used as money throughout Africa: 15,195 finely worked carnelian beads, 60,000 crystal stones, and 17 kilograms of cowrie shells.

There was big money to be made selling slaves in New World markets such as Cuba. In *Revelations of a Slave Smuggler,* Captain Richard Drake described the profits to be made from his shipload of slaves. "By actual calculation the average cost per head of the 350 blacks was $16, and in Havana the market average was $360, yielding a net profit, if safely delivered, of $120,400 for the cargo, from which should be deducted about $20,000 as the average cost of the clipper ship's round trip, including commissions. This would mark her earnings for the voyage, as about $100,000. Such were the enormous profits of the slave trade in 1835."

In the United States in 1845, a healthy eighteen-year-old boy sold at auction for around 650 dollars. Five years later that same slave would have sold for 1,000 dollars; the expenses of the slave trade had risen, as had demand. In 1860, just before the Civil War, slave prices doubled and a healthy male was worth 2,000 dollars. Slave values varied widely, as they have throughout history, depending on the age, skill, and health of the person being sold. The appraisers of one Alabama plantation owner's estate put a value of only 250 dollars on a young boy named Elbert and no value at all on an old man named Chester. The same appraisers valued one horse and three mules at 320 dollars.

Elbert, on the left, had an appraised value of 250 dollars. Chester, on the right, was considered to be worth nothing.

Today a slave laborer might be paid less than a dollar a day. In Pakistan, ten-year-old children stitch together soccer balls in a dirty factory ten to twelve hours a day. Though these children aren't auctioned off like slaves, their parents are so desperately poor that they feel they have no choice but to send their children off to a factory with the hope that their meager pay will help the family stave off starvation.

Whole families are lured into slavery in the deep forests of northeast Brazil. They are promised five dollars a day to clear the forest and burn the lumber to make charcoal, which is needed in vast quantities for the steel industry. But once they climb onto the trucks that take them far into the jungle, they are no different than slaves. Taken a thousand miles from their homes, they are put to work in one of the thousands of hot and dirty charcoal kilns. Their wages are eaten up by outrageous charges for food, drink, and transportation, and because they are so deep in the jungle, escape is impossible. Regular beatings by armed overseers make their lives no better than plantation slaves' lives a century ago.

In Sudan slavery not only still exists but is both widespread and organized. The victims are usually women and children, often Christians, who are taken by force from their homes in southern Sudan by Arab tribal militias. They are beaten and starved as they are driven to cities in the north. Then they are sold, given Arab names by their new owners, and forced to convert to Islam. All this is condoned by Sudan's militant Islamic government. A United Nations human rights monitor testified in U.S. congressional hearings that slaves are sold in open markets; in 1995 an American doctor witnessed people being sold for as little as fifteen dollars.

Father and son load a charcoal kiln in the forests of northeast Brazil.

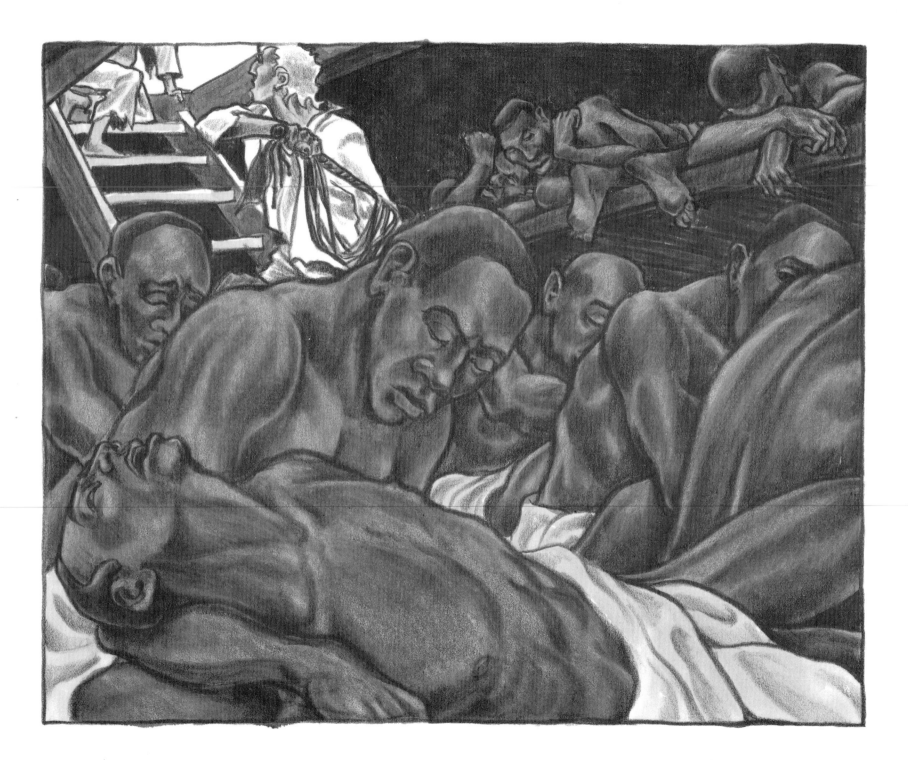

THE MIDDLE PASSAGE
& THE TRIANGLE TRADE

The dreaded Middle Passage was the second of three trips necessary to complete one cycle of the American slave trade. The first passage was the trip from Europe to the African coast with trade goods to exchange for slaves. The second, the middle passage, carried the slaves to the Americas. The third passage took the products and profits earned in trade back to Europe.

No matter the type of ship used, the experience for the slaves was the same. The men were chained together and packed into the cargo hold below deck. During the day, in good weather, most captains allowed the slaves up on deck. Women and children were allowed more freedom of movement but were seldom aboard slave ships in large numbers. Men typically outnumbered women two to one, and children rarely made up more than 10 percent of any shipment. There were reasons for the much larger numbers of men: Buyers in the New World wanted strong young men who could be put to work as soon as they landed, and African slavers preferred to keep the women and children to use as domestic slaves in their own households, so fewer were available to export. The food given to the slaves was usually bad, if not rotten, and the water was foul. Two meals a

opposite: The hold of a slave ship during the Middle Passage.

Cruelty and abuse were everyday realities aboard a slave ship.

day was typical. Manioc (a starchy root), yams, rice, cornmeal, or boiled beans were ladled out into the slaves' desperate hands. What they got depended on where in Africa the ship took on its cargo. If yams were the cheapest food available locally, then that's what the slaves ate.

During the Middle Passage it was commonplace for the ships' crews to brutally abuse the slaves. Slaves were whipped for no reason at all. The women and girls were sexually assaulted. Any slave who failed to do as he or she was told could be killed on the spot or thrown alive into the sea. After months of sickness, starvation, beatings, and sexual abuse, many slaves simply couldn't face further abuse. Some committed suicide by leaping overboard, others fell into a state of shock.

Disease was rampant on the slave ships. It was the leading cause of death during the Middle Passage. The European crews and African cargo were trapped together on a tiny ship in filthy conditions for weeks at a time. There were no toilets; one or two wooden buckets below deck were supposed to serve every slave on board. It was common knowledge that seamen could smell a slave ship five miles away if they were downwind of it. Making matters worse was the fact that whites and blacks had no immunity to each other's native diseases. Smallpox or dysentery could kill half the slaves during a voyage. Measles, malaria, and scurvy plagued slave ships, too. And disease is colorblind, so the European crews died just as quickly as their African prisoners did. Shipping records show that the death rate for the crews was as high as, and sometimes higher than, that of the slaves. Reports of events aboard ships making the Middle Passage are not always reliable, but a 15 percent death rate was probably typical. In a few notorious cases, the death rate among the slaves was much worse. In 1716, for example, 216 of 380 slaves aboard the *Windsor* died on their way to Brazil. In 1781, the captain of the *Zong* lost 60 of his 440 slaves bound for the West Indies and another 132 were so sick that he ordered them thrown overboard to collect on an insurance policy that paid for cargo lost at sea.

By the late 1700s, the British controlled much of the slave trade and conditions aboard their ships improved, relatively speaking. The death rate dropped to around 5 percent for several reasons. For one, fewer slaves were loaded on each ship, which improved the comfort level of the slaves, however slightly, and increased the number of survivors. Also, citrus fruits, which prevented scurvy, began to be part of the diet aboard ship. But perhaps the most important reason for the drop in mortality was the realization that the quicker the trip, the more people survived, slave and crew alike.

Another grim fate could await the slaves aboard a ship intercepted by a warship searching for illegal slave smugglers. If the captain of the slaver thought he was about to be captured, he might order the evidence of his crime destroyed to save himself and his crew from prison or the hangman's noose. The evidence, of course, was the slaves, and on numerous occasions they were pitched into the sea. One captain ordered the leg irons of the slaves clamped onto the anchor chain, then he ordered the anchor to be dropped into the sea, dragging all the slaves screaming under the waves. This way no bodies floated to the surface. When the ship was boarded by the English sailors, they found unused leg irons, whips, and even the smell of human captives, but the cargo hold was completely empty.

When a slave ship reached its destination, the slaves who were still alive got extra food and water and a bath, not out of kindness, but to prepare them for sale. Right before landing they were smeared with palm oil to give their skin a healthy shine, and older slaves had their gray hair dyed black or shaved off. Once on shore they were faced with another auction.

When the wealthy merchants of Rhode Island and Massachusetts began the

Before authorities boarded, slave smugglers often threw their human cargo into the sea to eliminate any evidence of illegal slave trading.

large-scale distillation of rum from the sugar and molasses of the West Indies in the eighteenth century, they had the final piece of one of the most lucrative business ventures in the colonies, the Triangle Trade. The process was simple: Take a cargo of New England rum, along with some other trade goods, and sail to the west coast of Africa. Trade the rum and trinkets for a load of slaves. Sail the Middle Passage to the West Indies and exchange the human cargo for barrels of molasses. Then make the third and last leg of the journey to deliver the molasses to New England to be made into more rum and start the process all over again. When viewed on a map of the Atlantic Ocean, these three trips form a triangle.

Newport, Bristol, and Providence, Rhode Island, were for a time the centers of the rum and slave business. In Newport alone there were twenty-two distilleries, and 15,000 barrels of rum were produced in Massachusetts in 1750. Rum and slavery were the most important products that came out of New England until after the American Revolution. At the time the Triangle Trade was considered a perfectly respectable and highly profitable line of work. Shipbuilders and distillers found not only financial gain, but convinced themselves they were doing God's work, too. They saw their efforts as a way to bring the light of Christianity to the poor Africans living in a heathen darkness.

The trade of barrels of rum for slaves was the foundation of the Triangle Trade.

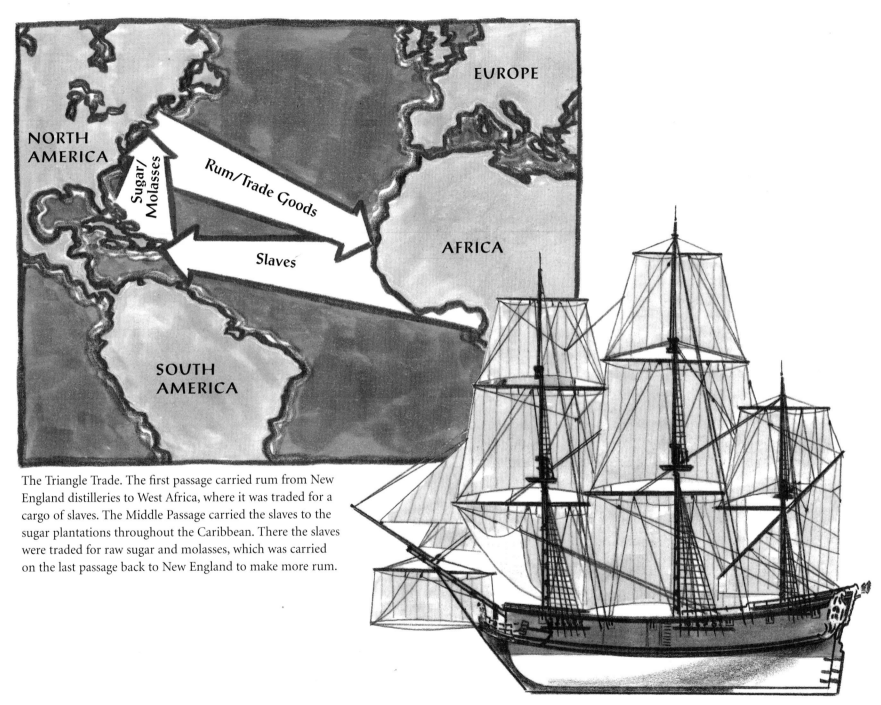

The Triangle Trade. The first passage carried rum from New England distilleries to West Africa, where it was traded for a cargo of slaves. The Middle Passage carried the slaves to the sugar plantations throughout the Caribbean. There the slaves were traded for raw sugar and molasses, which was carried on the last passage back to New England to make more rum.

A typical slave ship, this three-masted square rigger could pack more than four hundred slaves into its cargo hold.

TOOLS OF THE SLAVE TRADE

The slave trade had its own unique equipment and procedures. Since it was the only business involving the buying and selling of human beings, it required unusual and specialized equipment to restrain and control unwilling captives and move them to market as efficiently as possible.

The whip is as old as the slave trade, and nearly every slave in history was on the receiving end of its lash at one time or another. For thousands of years, the master or overseer was judge, jury, and executioner, and the whip was the law enforcement tool of choice. Whips were a common tool used to control livestock, particularly cattle and horses, but special whips were created for human beings. An American slave named John Brown described in detail the whip used on him and the other slaves on his plantation. "First a stock is chosen of a convenient length, the butt end of which is loaded with lead, to give the whip force. The stock is then cleverly split to within a foot or so of the butt, into twelve strips. A piece of tanned leather is then drawn on the stock so that the split lengths can be plaited together. This is done very regularly, until the leather tapers down to quite a fine point, the whip being altogether about six feet long, and as limber

opposite: The whip has been used on the backs of slaves for thousands of years.

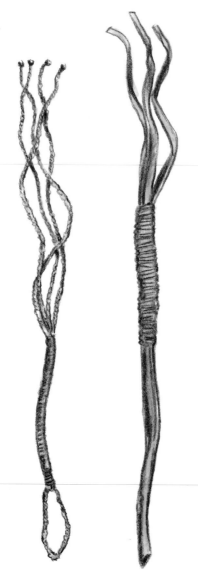

Two types of whips used to drive slaves.

and lithesome as a snake. The thong does not bruise but cuts; and those that are expert in the use of it can do so with such dexterity as to only raise the skin and draw blood or cut clean through to the bone. . . . The way of using it is to whirl it around until the thong acquires a certain forward power, and then to let the end of the thong fall across the back, the arm being drawn back with a kind of sweep. But although it is so formidable an instrument, it is seldom employed on slaves in such a manner as to disable them."

The *coffle,* which is the Arabic word for caravan, is the most prominent, identifiable image of slavery; a long line of human beings tied or chained together, trudging off to some distant place into a life of bondage. Simple cord or rope served most of the time. At the height of the trade in African slaves long pieces of wood with forked branches at each end served as the best form of restraint— a slave bound around the neck in the fork at each end. This was much cheaper than iron chains. Once securely restrained, slaves were marched to one of the many trading centers on the coastlines all around Africa. The march could take weeks, perhaps even months, depending on where the captives were taken. There is no way to tell how many died on the march to the sea, but eyewitness accounts suggest that the losses were heavy, perhaps even higher than losses aboard the slave ships.

Guns were certainly one of the most effective tools in the slave trade. The English exported more than 300,000 guns a year to Africa at the end of the eighteenth century. Guns and gunpowder quickly became indispensable to the slave trade because they were effective tools for acquiring prisoners. Slaves were traded for guns, which were then used to capture more slaves, which bought more guns, and so on, in a never-ending, vicious cycle. Africans captured and sold their countrymen so they could acquire weapons to protect themselves from anyone that tried to capture *them* to sell as slaves.

Professional slave hunters were an essential part of the slave trade; without them there would be no slaves to sell. Slave traders expanded their operations by employing slave hunters to pick potential targets and organize kidnapping raids. Sometimes a raiding party would set fire to a village and grab anyone who escaped the flames. As the demand for slaves for the transatlantic market grew, whole tribes became involved in slave hunting, abandoning their traditional livelihood in favor of the lucrative trade in people.

In 1481 the Portuguese built the first of many fortresses along the African coast at Elmina, in what is now Ghana. It was used primarily as a warehouse for slaves before they were loaded on ships bound for the New World. This massive symbol of Portuguese power had walls thirty feet thick topped by four hundred cannons. The cells inside could hold 1,000 people. Between 1500 and 1535 the Portuguese bought between 10,000 and 12,000 Africans at Elmina. The French, English, and Dutch followed and built their own fortresses up and down the western coast of Africa.

These European fortresses were built to protect the nearby slave factory, which was a temporary holding facility. These factories usually included a trading station, living quarters for the *factor* (the agent in charge of the slave-trading operation, he was usually European but not always), storage for trade goods, and repair shops for visiting slave ships. The buildings that held the slaves until the arrival of a slave ship could be simple huts with thatched roofs or large warehouses; they were called *barracoons.* The local African rulers granted permission to the European traders to build the barracoons and fortresses, charged the Europeans rent, and maintained control over them. This arrangement worked for both partners. The Europeans had a safe place to conduct business, haggle over prices, and inspect the human merchandise at their leisure; the Africans earned huge profits from the sale of the slaves they captured as well as the protection of the well-armed fortresses of their European business partners.

The conditions at the barracoons offered no relief for the slaves. They arrived

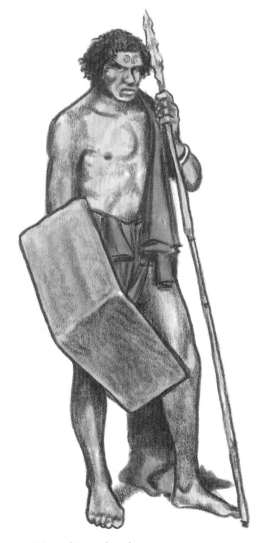

A West African slave hunter.

A slave hesitates before passing through the Door of No Return.

starved, beaten, and no doubt severely depressed, and their health and spirits were not likely to improve during their stay. Two miles off the coast of Dakar, the capital of Senegal, lies Goree Island. There were more than one hundred barracoons on this tiny sixty-five-acre island. The most infamous of these houses was La Maison des Ensclaves (the House of the Slaves), which exists today as a museum of the horrors of slavery. As many as 400 slaves were held in this small two-story house for several months waiting for the next slave ship to arrive. Inside was a courtyard that led to a series of dark cells. Up to thirty people were chained to the walls in each of these rooms. Men, women, and children were separated. Members of the same family or tribe were split up to minimize the risk of organized resistance. When a slave ship arrived, the slaves were assembled in the courtyard to be weighed and inspected. Those who were sold were branded with a hot iron with the buyer's mark or number, then lined up in front of a heavy door called the door of no return. Once the slaves passed through this door they would never see their African homeland again. When the door was opened, it revealed a narrow wooden gangplank that stretched two hundred feet from the door, across the beach, and onto the deck of the slave ship. It must have been a terrifying moment for everyone who passed through that door. The barked orders of the drivers—long-haired white men who were rumored to be cannibals—the crack of their whips, the horrible screams, and the black silhouette of a strange ship in the bright sun was overwhelming for some. They couldn't take any more and flung themselves into the shark-infested waters.

Those who resisted the temptation to leap into the sea may have regretted their decision when faced with conditions on board the ship that would be their home for the next several weeks or even months. The voyage from Goree to the Caribbean might take three weeks. The trip from other slave factories farther down Africa's coast might take several months, depending on their destination.

Ships of every conceivable kind were used to transport slaves, but those ships that were specially designed to carry as much human cargo as possible were the most profitable. Slave ships were either loose packed or tight packed. A loosely packed ship of average size (about 200 tons) might carry 400 slaves. A tightly packed ship of the same size could carry up to 700 slaves. On ships of this period there was usually no more than a five-foot-high cargo hold. The tight packers custom fitted their ships with shelves that stretched the whole length of the cargo hold on both sides; it cut the space in half but nearly doubled the number of slaves that could be crammed on board. This gave each person a space 6 feet long, 16 inches wide, and just 2½ feet high. On some ships people couldn't move from that space for the whole voyage. Captains learned to make it a priority to reach the closest slave market as quickly as possible. Shipbuilding technology also helped, providing slavers with faster ships. Slaves who survived the ordeal of the Middle Passage, though, had little to look forward to in the New World.

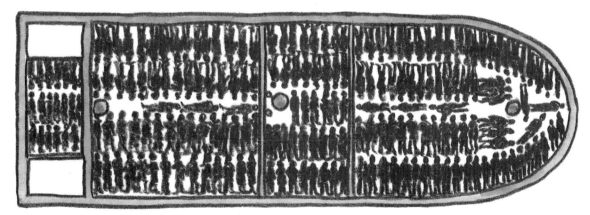

This diagram shows how slaves were packed onto ships.

THE TREATMENT OF
SLAVES & THE LAW

In Babylon in the eighteenth century B.C. the treatment of slaves ranged from simple cruelty to open-minded tolerance. The laws governing slaves and their status were similar in all the early Middle Eastern cultures. Slaves were legally defined as property and were even branded, like cattle, with a red-hot iron. Their masters could sell them at their discretion, choose their mates, and they automatically owned any children born to their slaves. Women and girls were often compelled to submit sexually to their owners and would remain slaves even after bearing his children. But in contrast to their legendary cruelty, both the Assyrians and later the Babylonians allowed some of their slaves a remarkable amount of independence—they could own land, property, even their own slaves. Industrious slaves could, with their masters' permission, run their own businesses, and records show that slaves held many important governmental positions.

Hammurabi of Babylon conquered all of Mesopotamia in the eighteenth century B.C. His code of laws was displayed on intricately carved slabs of stone, or stelae, in temples throughout his empire. One of these, a slab of basalt eight feet tall, is now in the Louvre Museum in Paris. On it are recorded three hundred

opposite: A Venetian slaveowner decides the fate of a slave girl caught stealing food from the master's kitchen.

laws that outline legal guidelines for almost every part of Babylonian life. Laws regarding slavery include: "If he has destroyed the eye of another man's slave or broken the bone of another's slave, he shall pay one-half his value." Hiding an escaped slave was not a good idea: "If a man has harbored in his house either a fugitive male or female slave belonging to the state or to a private citizen and has not brought him forth at the summons of the police, the householder shall be put to death." Penalties for failing to follow Hammurabi's code for even the simplest business deal were severe: "If a man has purchased or he has received for safekeeping either silver or gold or a male slave or a female slave or an ox or a sheep or an ass or anything from the hand of another man's son or a man's slave without witnesses and contracts, since that man is a thief, he shall be put to death."

Although some Roman slaves enjoyed luxurious lives, held important positions in government, and moved freely throughout the empire, in the eyes of Roman law, they had no more civil or human rights than the most abused field slave. The law made clear that the master's rights over his slave were absolute. Even when laws were passed later in the empire that recognized some basic human rights, slaves were at the mercy of their owners throughout all of Roman history. Punishments for uncooperative slaves could be harsh. Minor misconduct might earn a slave a trip to the stocks. The most common punishment was whipping. If a special whip was used that had sharp pieces of metal tied along its length, a lashing could kill a man. Slaves, though, feared a sentence of hard labor more than the whip. However brutal a flogging was, it was over quickly. But a sentence to hard labor in a mine or a quarry, especially for a spoiled city slave, was considered a fate worse than death, particularly since in the Roman mines, death was almost always part of the bargain. You simply worked until you died. A sentence to a Roman galley (a large ship propelled by sails and oars) was dreaded almost as much. Capital punishment was widespread, and for the

Crucifixion was the fate of Roman slaves convicted of a serious crime.

Roman slave a death sentence was typically carried out by crucifixion, a verdict passed down by the criminal courts for offenses such as theft, assault, murder, and rebellion. Another popular way to kill unruly slaves was to throw them to the beasts in the amphitheater during the games. Slaves who had a bad attitude but showed promise as fighters were often sold to a gladiator school, where they would be trained to fight in the arena. If a gladiator was skilled or lucky enough to win lots of fights, he could become rich; if he was very lucky, he could be awarded his freedom. Many won their freedom but were lured back into the arena by large cash prizes.

Many Roman slaves fought for their lives as gladiators.

In the Islamic world, most slaves were used in private homes and shops and were generally treated well; in many cases they came to be part of their owner's family. The slavery practiced in some African cultures could also be described as humane. Slaves, be they prisoners of war, debtors, or even criminals, maintained a close relationship with their masters. Master and slave shared chores, although the slave was assigned the harder work. Their children played together, and marriage between them was common. But no matter how kind the master was, his slaves had been taken by force from their homes and were there against their will. And there are plenty of examples of cruelty: One king of Dahomey ordered two slaves beheaded every morning to give thanks for a good night's sleep. The sacrifice of slaves was not at all uncommon.

Aztec slaves in the sixteenth century, called *tlacotin,* occupied the lowest place in Aztec society but fared far better than slaves in other cultures. They were rarely mistreated and retained some important individual rights, such as the right to marry whomever they pleased and to own property. They were commonly allowed to live in their own houses. To the Aztecs, slavery was a condition that could strike anybody and was sometimes only a temporary predicament. But in spite of the milder elements of Aztec slavery, slaves still could be worked hard and treated roughly. Aztec slaves were domestic servants for the nobility or served as laborers. Since Mesoamerica (Mexico and Central America) had no horses, oxen, or mules until they were introduced by the Spanish, people were used as beasts of burden. Slaves carried all of the produce, trade goods, and tribute payments along the extensive trade routes across the Aztec empire. Slaves who were troublemakers got three chances to straighten up. If they didn't, they were then sold to the priests to be sacrificed.

Civilizations with vast urban centers filled with thousands of people didn't exist in North America before the eighteenth century, but slavery did. Many Native North American tribes kept slaves. In some cases, slaves were routinely brutalized, killed, and occasionally eaten, but in other cases, slaves were adopted by their masters and fully integrated into tribal society. Slaves taken by many North American Indian tribes were eventually adopted by the tribes and suffered no social stigma from their former slave status. In other tribes slaves were barely fed, and if they died, they were literally thrown away, into the sea or an open pit. They could be bought, sold, given away, or killed at the whim of their masters. In many of these tribes, slaves were an individual's most important possessions. A good female slave was more valuable than a wife who had no powerful family connections. Being such a valuable possession did not guarantee a slave's safety. On the contrary, Northwest Indians sacrificed slaves as a demonstration of their wealth and status. During the ceremony to dedicate the construction of a new longhouse, a slave was crushed beneath the central pillar. The Kwakiutl Indians ate their sacrificial victims. Wealthy chiefs celebrated important events, such as a birth or a marriage, with a potlatch, a great feast. To show off the family's prestige, expensive gifts were given to the guests and a favorite slave was sacrificed with a special ceremonial club called, appropriately, the slave killer. Wealthy Chinooks, who lived along the lower Columbia River (which flows through British Columbia in Canada and Washington and Oregon in the U.S.) and were also aggressive slave traders, staked a slave to the grave of a family member and left him or her to starve to death in the belief that the slave could serve the departed one in the next life.

JOHN R. JEWITT

John R. Jewitt was hired as the armorer aboard the brig Boston. *He set sail from England on March 2, 1802, bound for the Pacific Northwest coast of North America to trade for furs. After a voyage of 190 days, his ship arrived at the Nootka Sound of Vancouver Island. The seemingly peaceful Indians traded with the Englishmen for*

John R. Jewitt.

Macquinna, chief of the Nootkas.

nearly two weeks, until the day before the ship was to leave. Then, without any warning, the Indians attacked, murdering every crew member they could catch. Within minutes Jewitt was surrounded by the bodies of his crewmates. He wrote in the journal he kept throughout the ordeal, "I now thought my last moment had come, and recommended my soul to my maker. The king, who, as I have already observed, knew enough of English to make himself understood, entered the circle, and placing himself before me, addressed me nearly in the following words— 'John—I speak—you no say no—You say no—daggers come!' He then asked me if I would be his slave during my life—If I would fight for him in his battles—If I would repair his muskets and make daggers and knives for him—with several other questions, to all of which I was careful to answer, yes. He then told me that he would spare my life, and ordered me to kiss his hands and feet to show my submission to him, which I did."

Jewitt spent the next two years as a captive of Macquinna, the remarkable chief of the Nootkas. He became a favorite of the chief and so was treated well. It also helped that he was smart enough to realize that he had little choice but to make the best of his predicament. He learned their language, observed their lifestyle, and recorded everything he saw in meticulous detail. Finally, in July of 1805, a ship arrived and Jewitt managed to trick his captors and escape. Once free he wrote, "I could not avoid experiencing a painful sensation on parting with this savage chief, who had preserved my life, and in general treated me with kindness..."

John Jewitt arrived in Boston in the summer of 1807. By the end of the year his journal had been published and his remarkable story proved to be a sensation with readers. He later turned his story into a musical with himself as the star. He performed in theaters up and down the East Coast. He died in 1821 in Hartford, Connecticut, at the age of thirty-seven. According to tribal historians, his captor, Macquinna, died sometime after 1825, leading a raid on a neighboring village.

The history of slavery is full of hideous accounts of cruelty to slaves. But official French records reveal acts of torture in colonial Haiti that are difficult to believe. Slaves were chained to a log or block of wood and forced to drag it behind them wherever they went. Tin masks or muzzles were locked over the faces of slaves caught eating the sugar cane. Salt, cinders, and hot ashes were rubbed into wounds after a whipping. Arms, legs, hands, feet, ears, and noses were cut off for minor infractions. Boiling cane sugar was poured over uncooperative slaves. They might be slowly roasted over a fire or buried up to their necks, their heads smeared with sugar to be eaten away by flies. One unfortunate victim was force-fed gunpowder, then blown up from the inside.

The life of a Haitian slave was cheap. So long as the sugar industry continued to generate huge profits, the barbaric treatment of slaves was ignored. The French royal government was concerned only with the revenue its colonies provided, not with the human rights of its slaves. There were no laws protecting slaves and the colonists could treat their slaves however they wished. The Catholic Church had a presence in Haiti but was not nearly as outspoken in regard to the treatment of slaves as it was in the Spanish and Portuguese colonies. Manumission, the term for legally giving a slave his or her freedom, was rare, and few slaves successfully bought their freedom. There was little hope for the slaves of Haiti. Suicide was common, but so were attacks on cruel masters. The only other option was to run away, which they did by the thousands.

In the southern United States, slave laws or the black code spelled out exactly what slaves were forbidden to do. Since most slaves were not taught to read or write, these codes served mostly to reinforce the complete mastery of the owner over his human property. According to these laws, slaves had no right to a trial by jury, they could not sue, they could make no contract, they could own no property, they could not inherit anything. Slaves couldn't travel without a pass, carry any weapon, gamble, smoke, or swear. These rules were enforced by the master according to his nature. A humane master ignored many of these laws. In 1850 the Fugitive Slave Act was passed. It allowed slaveowners to pursue and capture escaped slaves, even in states and territories where slavery was prohibited. Federal marshals earned a fee for every slave returned to his or her owners. This system rewarded unscrupulous marshals who captured free blacks and collected their fee based on phony claims of ownership. The Dred Scott decision of the Supreme Court in 1857 deepened the country's division on the issue of slavery. The court ruled that a runaway slave, even if he or she reached a state where slavery was illegal, was not legally free. As the nation expanded westward, there was intense debate over whether the new territories should be slave states or free states. The United States was split between the free Northern states and the slaveholding Southern states.

Even in the nineteenth century after slavery had been abolished in many parts of the world, there were places where slavery thrived and its practice was as brutal as it had been anywhere in the past. In describing a slave caravan in Zanzibar in the late 1800s, a British missionary wrote: "It is difficult to adequately describe the filthy state of their bodies; in many instances not only scarred by the cut of a '*chikote*' [a piece of hide used as a whip] but feet and shoulders were a mass of open sores, made more painful by the swarms of flies which followed the march and lived on the flowing blood. They presented a moving picture of utter misery, and one could not help wondering how any of them survived the long tramp from the Upper Congo, at least 1,000 miles distant. . . . The head-men in charge were most polite to us as they passed our camp. Each was armed with a rifle, a knife, and spear, and although decently clothed in clean cotton garments, they presented a thoroughly villainous appearance. Addressing one, I pointed out that many of the slaves were unfit to carry loads. To this he smilingly replied 'They have no choice! They must go, or die!' Then ensued the following conversation:

'What do you do if they become too ill to travel?' 'Spear them at once!' was the fiendish reply. . . . 'I see women carrying not only a child . . . but in addition, a tusk of ivory or other burden. . . . What do you do in their case when they become too weak to carry both? . . . Who carries the ivory?' 'She does! We cannot leave valuable ivory on the road. We spear the child and make her burden lighter. Ivory first, child afterwards!'"

The treatment of slaves throughout history varied according to the conscience of their masters, the customs of the society in which they lived, and the degree of economic dependence on their labor. There were always masters who treated their slaves kindly and provided plenty of food, decent clothing and shelter, and a reasonable amount of work. Some slaves were lucky enough to be loved as a member of their owner's family. Others were treated worse than any farm animal. Most laws regarding slavery were written to protect the investment of the owner, not the rights of the slave. Those laws that dealt with the humane treatment of slaves were written to prevent only the worst abuses and to lessen any chance of rebellion.

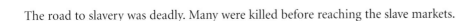

The road to slavery was deadly. Many were killed before reaching the slave markets.

TYPES OF SLAVE LABOR

Over the centuries more slaves have probably been used as domestic servants than as any other kind of laborers. Cooking, cleaning, child care, chopping wood, fetching water, and other household chores were a slave's major tasks in most cultures, beginning with ancient Mesopotamia. In the Roman Empire during the reign of Augustus, the richest 5 percent of the population owned 1 million house slaves.

A typical wealthy Roman household had dozens, maybe hundreds of slaves for every conceivable task. There was a full kitchen staff, a laundry staff, a cleaning staff, a slave to shave the master every morning, another to wash his feet, and another to set out his clothes. Some rich Romans had a special slave whose sole purpose was to guard the front door, and he could be counted on to be there at all times because he was chained to it like a dog. When the master or any member of his family went into the city for a little shopping, they wouldn't consider walking; that was for mere plebeians, the common people. They would be carried through the streets on a litter, a chair borne on the shoulders of specially dressed slaves, often from Syria or Cappadocia, who were considered the litter-bearers of choice for the wealthy Roman.

opposite: Slaves working a gold mine in colonial Brazil.

The house of Calvus left a good record of how slaves were used in a rich Roman's house: The slave staff was called the *familia urbana,* the city household, and it consisted of some one hundred and fifty people, all slaves. The *procurator,* named Cleander, was responsible for all purchasing and all business outside the household. Reporting to Cleander were the *dispesator,* who managed all the stockrooms and supplies, the *atriensis,* who oversaw the day-to-day operations, and the *sileniarius,* who enforced discipline and was responsible for security. The rest of the staff was split into *decuria,* groups of ten, each under a team leader and each responsible for a specific task. There were the cleaners, the kitchen staff, the serving staff, the chambermaids (and boys), the wardrobe attendants, the master's personal valet, maids for the lady of the house, the children's attendants, a troop of messengers, and litter-bearers. There were also four secretaries— two devoted to the master's businesses and two to handle domestic affairs—a librarian, and two physicians who dealt mostly with the *familia* but occasionally treated the minor illnesses of the master and his family. The staff was equally balanced, male and female, and there were numerous married couples.

Slaves ran most city services in Rome. They maintained all public buildings, served state officials (who were often slaves themselves), and assisted the temple priests. Slaves served as Rome's firemen, jailers, and executioners and provided most of its notorious public entertainments. Musicians, acrobats, animal trainers, chariot drivers, and gladiators were either bought specifically for their particular talents or were trained in either government or private schools dedicated to their craft. It should be noted that free men and women performed these roles, too, and even volunteered to fight as gladiators. Some of these entertainers, notably famous chariot drivers and champion gladiators, slave or not, were richer than all but the richest free Romans.

Agriculture used a lot of slave labor. Virtually all of Rome's agricultural production was done by slaves. Commercial crops that required a great deal of labor to plant, tend, and harvest, such as olives, grapes, rice, tobacco, sugar, and cotton, were popular with slaveowners. Romans used a lot of slaves in olive groves and vineyards, and some African societies depended on slaves to cultivate coffee and rice along with coconuts, cloves, and peanuts. The vast sugar plantations of the New World, especially in Brazil, used millions of slaves. The plantation system of gang labor could produce tons of sugar cheaply, and that meant big profits could be made in Europe, where sugar was in great demand. It was a matter of scale; the bigger the plantation, the larger the sugar crop, enabling larger profits but demanding more slaves. Sugar cane was introduced to Brazil by the Portuguese in 1540. By 1580 there were sixty sugar mills operating, and they required great quantities of cut sugar cane to keep them working and large numbers of slaves to do the cutting. The native Indians were originally supposed to do the work, but the brutal conditions imposed by their new Portuguese masters killed off most of them. Of 40,000 Indians who were enslaved in the Bahia region of Brazil in 1563, all but 3,000 were dead twenty years later. The Europeans found ample replacements in Africa. Five out of every six Africans sent to Brazil ended up working on its huge plantations that produced cacao, coffee, and cotton in addition to sugar. One coffee planter admitted that he expected to get only one year's worth of labor out of a slave before he died, but he factored that into his expenses so he could still show a profit. It was typical to expect only twenty-five out of every hundred slaves to survive three years. Slaves were cheap; machines, oxen, and mules were expensive.

The cotton plantations of the American South needed lots of slaves because cotton was such a labor-intensive crop.

WORKING THE COTTON FIELDS

Solomon Northup described in detail the process of cultivating cotton. First the field was plowed. A slave girl usually followed behind the plow, dropping seed, followed by another plow that covered the seed. Throughout the blistering heat of the Louisiana summer, the rows of cotton were hoed by gangs of slaves four different times. Northup writes: "The overseer or driver follows the slaves on horseback with a whip. . . . The fastest hoer takes the lead row. He is usually about a rod (five and a half yards) in advance of his companions. If one of them passes him, he is whipped. If one falls behind or is a moment idle, he is whipped. In fact, the lash is flying from morning till night, the whole day long. The hoeing season thus continues from April until July, a field having no sooner been finished once, than it is commenced again.

"In the later part of August begins the cotton picking season. At this time each

slave is presented with a sack. Each one is also presented with a large basket that will hold about two barrels. This is to put the cotton in when the sack is filled . . .

"An ordinary day's work is two hundred pounds. A slave who is accustomed to picking is punished, if he or she brings in a less quantity than that . . .

"The cotton grows from five to seven feet high, each stalk having a great many branches, shooting out in all directions, and lapping each other above the water furrow.

"Sometimes the slave picks down one side of a row, and back upon the other, but more usually, there is one on either side, gathering all that has blossomed, leaving the unopened bolls for a succeeding picking. When the sack is filled, it is emptied into the basket and trodden down."

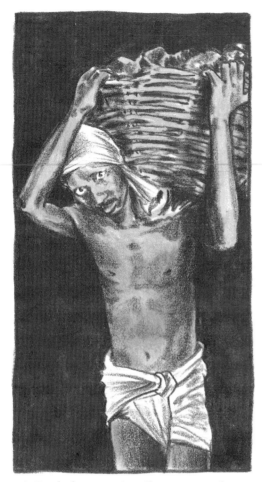

A Greek slave carrying silver ore out of a mine in the Laurium hills, near Athens.

Hard physical labor was not limited to the fields. Mining had the highest death rate of any slave occupation, and the short working life of those forced into the mines necessitated lots of replacements. Silver was discovered near Athens in the hills of Laurium around 55 B.C. The Athenian government owned the mines and leased mining rights to private contractors. Some mine operators owned their own slave labor force; others rented them from slave dealers. At one time there were 30,000 slaves working in the mines and processing plants. The silver brought out of the mines by all those slaves fueled Athens's prosperity, which, ironically, allowed the development of Greek democracy.

European conquerors forced thousands of Native Americans and Africans into mines throughout Central and South America, as did the rulers of the African kingdoms of Ghana and Mali. From the 1920s through the 1950s, millions of people were worked to death in the coal and gold mines in the labor camps called gulags in the Soviet Union. These people weren't slaves in the traditional sense, in that they were neither bought nor sold. They were political prisoners or dissidents (someone who disagreed with the communist government) who were arrested and then sentenced to slave labor. Other forms of hard labor in the gulags were lumber production and construction projects. All of Rome's massive construction projects—amphitheaters for the games, aqueducts for fresh water, government buildings, and temples for worshipping the many gods were built by countless thousands of slave laborers. The skilled workmen were slaves, too—the carpenters, stonemasons, and bricklayers—as were the architects and engineers who designed all these impressive public structures.

Many slaves ended their lives pulling an oar on a galley. These ships were propelled through the water by oars and required the rowing power of hundreds of men. This form of slave labor was not as common in the ancient world as it was during the Middle Ages. The Barbary States and the Ottoman Empire used lots of slaves to propel their fleets, especially Slavs taken in raids from around the

Crimean peninsula in the Mediterranean Sea. The Islamic city-states of Algeria, Morocco, Tunisia, and Tripolitania, known as the Barbary States, inundated the sea with war galleys looking for plunder and slaves. These slave-powered ships went through large numbers of men. Unless a slave was in excellent physical condition, he wouldn't survive for long. The oarsmen on these galleys didn't sit on benches, as was the practice in the galleys in ancient times. They stood and had to lunge forward on the oar, putting their whole bodies into the stroke to propel the ship. The whip of the overseer encouraged maximum effort.

Besides hard physical labor, sexual slavery was and still is one of slavery's worst occupations. Forced prostitution was commonplace in the earliest civilizations and continues to this day. Female slaves have always been subjected to concubinage, the practice of using a female slave for sex. Large groups of concubines, known as harems, were common among the wealthy classes all over the Islamic world. Muslim women could own slaves, but they lived in a completely male-dominated society, so they were forbidden sexual access to male slaves. In some cultures, the children born of a relationship between a free man and his concubine were considered free; in others, the concubine was freed also. Ancient Rome and the American South were unique in that concubines and their children were never set free. In African societies concubines were used principally to continue the family line; consequently, concubines and their children were adopted into the master's family.

Eunuchs, castrated male slaves, were used to guard the harems, ensuring that only the master could use his concubines. Only about ten percent of men survived the crude surgery that removed their testicles, but among those who did, many ultimately attained powerful positions. Eunuchs were also private servants of the wealthy palace staff members, and they maintained the sacred places of Islam, the mosques and tombs.

Luckier slaves were employed in skilled trades or as merchants. The carpenters,

Galley slaves.

blacksmiths, masons, tailors, and weavers of Rome, Medieval Europe, and Mesopotamia were often slaves. Slaves were used in family businesses beginning in ancient Babylonia and continuing in Greece, Rome, Africa, the Islamic world, and Italy in the Middle Ages. In some cases they were allowed a great deal of freedom and entrusted with large sums of money. Two Greek slaves, Pasion and Pharmio, were among the richest men in Athens at one time. On the other hand, slaves in the American South were never allowed to operate businesses.

Temple slaves of the Aztecs and the Mayas enjoyed very high status, at least if they could avoid being sacrificed to the gods. The Aztecs used slaves taken as prisoners of war for human sacrifices. Aztec religious rituals required human blood, and lots of it. Cutting the heart out of living victims was a common form of sacrifice that was unique to Mesoamerica. The Aztecs believed that unless they offered human hearts and blood to their gods, the sun would disappear. As many as 20,000 people were executed on the stone altars of Aztec temples every year. The constant intertribal warfare and raids on neighboring cities were as necessary to satisfy the thirst for sacrificial victims as they were for political or strategic reasons.

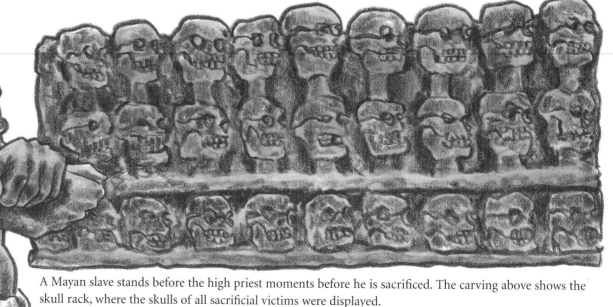

A Mayan slave stands before the high priest moments before he is sacrificed. The carving above shows the skull rack, where the skulls of all sacrificial victims were displayed.

Sacrifice also played a major role in Mayan religion. The Mayas built a great empire that ruled over large areas of southern Mexico and parts of Central America. Their civilization was at its peak between 600 and 900 A.D. Animals—iguanas, turtles, dogs, wild boars, and jaguars—were frequently used as offerings to the gods. People were sacrificed, too. Their blood was believed essential to the health and prosperity of Mayan culture. Like the Aztecs, constant warfare among neighboring tribes ensured an ample supply of sacrificial slaves. High-ranking prisoners of war were especially prized as sacrifices; the ritual killing of a powerful enemy made the sacrifice more potent and more pleasing to the gods. Children were also valued as sacrifices because of their innocence and purity. Orphans were used, as were children from neighboring cities who were taken in raids or were bought by the priests in order to be killed.

This carving shows the sacrificial stone upon which the slave will be killed.

A *mamluk* warrior.

Slaves were commonly used as soldiers; in fact, societies that refused to use slaves in combat were rare. Only in the Athenian navy, the infantry legions of Rome, and the Confederate army in the Civil War were slaves refused service. But when the military situation became desperate, that prohibition was quickly forgotten and slaves were armed and sent into battle. In many other cultures, slave soldiers reached very high status, some rising to command armies or run entire countries.

MAMLUKS AND JANISSARIES: SLAVE WARRIORS

Mamluk *is an Arabic word meaning "one who is owned." Technically, it refers to a slave soldier who was taken as a boy, trained in warfare, converted to Islam, and pressed into service. Many* mamluks *remained slaves throughout their entire careers, no matter how high their rank or powerful their office. Some, however, were freed when their training was complete.*

Since according to Islamic law only non-Muslims could be enslaved, mamluks *came from every non-Muslim territory that surrounded the Islamic world: sub-Saharan Africa, Slavic Europe, Anatolia (now part of Turkey), the Caucasus (the mountain region of southeastern Europe), and primarily the vast plains of western Asia. Tartars, the Turkic tribesmen who lived there, were prized by the Arabs for their toughness, pride, and remarkable skill as mounted archers.*

During the late Middle Ages, the armies of Egypt were made up entirely of slave soldiers. These mamluks, *like those in Iraq, were Slavs and Tartars bought in markets around the Black Sea and shipped by Muslim traders to Egypt. In 1250* mamluk *troops assassinated the Egyptian caliph and took over. The Mamluk sultans ruled for more than two hundred fifty years, until 1517. By that time they had evolved into an aristocratic warrior class, although throughout their reign they depended heavily on foreign slaves to fill the army.*

The Ottoman Empire was named after Osman I, a Turkish chieftain who united northwest Turkey under Muslim control in the thirteenth century. In the following centuries it grew into an Islamic empire that ruled all of Asia Minor, the Balkans, the Crimea, Hungary, and parts of North Africa, Arabia, and Syria. The Ottoman Empire was the most slavery-dependent culture until the pre–Civil War southern United States.

The Ottoman infantry was called the Janissaries. Like the mamluks, they were slaves, taken as children and trained to be Islamic warriors. From roughly 1400 through most of the 1600s the primary source for the Janissaries was the devshirme, a periodic levying of Christian boys for military training. After years of intense instruction they entered the ranks of the Janissaries, who were among the best trained and most disciplined fighting forces of the Middle Ages. Their fierce loyalty and formidable fighting skills were an important factor in the Ottoman Empire's military success. Their distinctive headgear—a foot-high white cap that folded down over the shoulders—became a symbol of Ottoman power.

A janissary, the elite warrior of the Ottoman Empire.

FREEDOM FROM SLAVERY

Slaves could be set free in many slaveholding societies. In some places, slaves were eventually set free after they served their sentence; in other places, slaves had no chance to be freed. Most societies allowed owners to free slaves whenever they wished. In ancient Mesopotamia a slave could be set free by his owner at any time, but such acts appear to have been rare. Sumerian slaves could marry free persons and any children produced by such a marriage were automatically free. Manumission was easy in the Roman Empire and happened all the time. It could be granted as a reward, or freedom could be bought by a slave himself. Freed Roman slaves wore caps on their heads as a symbol of their freedom. They no longer belonged to their master but continued to have a strong relationship with him. They would usually continue to assist their former master in his business or rely on him to finance a new business enterprise.

In the Middle Ages, the Catholic Church encouraged manumission as an act of mercy. The freedom of an English dairy maid was bought in the following will: "Here it is made known in this gospel that Godwin the Buck has bought Leofgifu the dairy maid at North Stoke and her offspring from Abbot Aelfsige

opposite: A slave is freed in North Africa after six years of servitude.

for half a pound, to eternal freedom, in the witness of all the community of Bath. Christ blind him who ever perverts this."

Islamic societies usually encouraged the manumission of slaves after a set period of servitude; six years was typical. Slaves who adopted Islam could also expect to be freed eventually. The prevalence of household slavery among Muslims contributed to the relative ease with which their slaves were granted freedom; the close relationships formed in the household eased the transition from foreign stranger to adopted family member.

Birth could be a path to freedom in some cultures; in others the rule was "born a slave, die a slave." Many African societies considered the offspring of slaves to be free; among them were the Dahomeans in West Africa and the Ashanti in Ghana. This was in part because of the influence of Islam but also because of the importance of ensuring the continuation of the family line. Making all slave children free and adopting them into the family greatly increased the chances of a long family history.

In the Americas, there were several places where manumission was easy. The Aztecs freed every child born to slaves, except those whose parents were condemned as traitors. For these children, the parents' offense meant a life of slavery; for the parents, death on the sacrificial altar.

A slave was much more likely to be set free in colonial Cuba than he was in other European colonies in the New World. Masters were encouraged by the Catholic Church to free their slaves; all that was required was an open declaration in church before a priest that the slave was free. The Cuban colonial government allowed slaves to buy their own freedom. This policy of *coartacion* allowed slaves to pay for their freedom on the installment plan. If a slave was worth five hundred dollars, he or she could make twenty payments of twenty-five dollars each to earn his freedom. Slaves earned the money to make these payments by selling the produce from their private gardens or working odd jobs on Sundays and holidays and saving their wages—after paying the master his cut. By 1877 more than half of Cuba's black population was made up of freed slaves and there was no social stigma attached to their ex-slave status. Cuba had long integrated Africans into the culture, so freed slaves enjoyed the full rights of all Cuban citizens. This experience proved to be vastly different from that of the slaves of the West Indies and North America. There manumission was extremely rare. The southern United States was unique among history's most slave-dependent societies in that manumission almost never happened. Granting slaves freedom was even forbidden by law in several states. Such laws were passed in South Carolina in 1820, Mississippi in 1822, Arkansas in 1858, and in both Alabama and Maryland in 1860. Occasionally slaves were manumitted in their masters' wills, but it was usually a loyal household slave who was set free. For the field hand or factory slave any chance of freedom seemed hopelessly remote.

ESCAPE!

Slaves ran away if they thought they could escape without getting caught. An especially brutal overseer or a brief lapse in security motivated many spontaneous attempts to flee, but planned escapes were undertaken more often, especially if a safe refuge was within reach or the slave could blend in with the free population.

There was a wide range of attitudes about runaway slaves in the ancient Middle East. At one extreme, Hammurabi's code demanded the death of the head of the household that sheltered a runaway; at the other end, the law of the ancient Hebrews granted runaways refuge. Escape was not uncommon in ancient Rome, but the empire was so vast that it was difficult to get outside its borders. Slave-owners employed professional bounty hunters to track down escaped slaves. When a slave was captured, he or she could be branded on the forehead with the letter "F" that stood for *fugitivus* (fugitive) or forced to wear a metal collar around the neck.

One law, found nowhere else in the history of slavery, allowed a runaway

opposite: A runaway slave hides from his pursuers.

Aztec slave to go free if he or she made it to the king's palace without being caught. If anyone but the owner's son interfered with the slave's run for freedom, that person had to take the slave's place.

The suffering on the plantations of colonial Brazil forced many to flee. Some ran for the cities and there attempted to pass themselves off as free. Others escaped to the jungle. Colonies of runaways, called *quilombos,* sprouted up throughout Brazil. Some thrived and became productive settlements with their own plantations run by a mixed population of blacks and Indians. Heavily armed bands of slave hunters employed by the planters searched the jungle for runaways. Those who were caught were branded and sent back to work. Those who were caught after running away a second time had an ear cut off. After a third unsuccessful escape, they were decapitated and their heads were put on display as a warning to other slaves.

Cuban slaves ran away in droves, too. The drudgery of life on a plantation was difficult to endure. Slaves were worked from sunrise to sunset, then packed into dingy, dirt-floored barracoons at night. The runaways formed into bands known as *cimarrones* and built stockaded villages called *palenques* in the mountains and swamps of Cuba's interior. The inhabitants of the *cimarrones* could eke out a living by farming and occasionally raiding nearby plantations. They traded with the pirates who prowled the waters around Cuba and took every opportunity to annoy the Spanish authorities.

In the United States, running away and staying free was very difficult. During the American Revolution, tens of thousands of slaves tried to run when their owners were preoccupied with the fight against the British. Conditions were so bad on plantations before the Civil War that slaves often felt that there were just two ways out: suicide or escape. Any attempt to run was risky. Gangs of professional slave catchers were everywhere. Slaves who were caught faced whipping, branding, or beating. Those with children might see them sold away as punishment. Even if a runaway made it to a free state, he or she had to be careful. Slave catchers roamed the free states searching for suspicious-looking blacks, and since to the slave catchers all black people looked suspicious, any of them, slave or free, could be kidnapped and sent south. Slave catchers were looking for reward money, not justice. Even law-abiding citizens were compelled to turn in runaways. Federal law forbade any aid for escaped slaves. Anyone caught providing food, shelter, or assistance of any kind could get six months in jail and a thousand-dollar fine.

The threat of jail or a fine couldn't stop those who were opposed to slavery from helping slaves escape. Free blacks and sympathetic whites secretly organized a network of hiding places and safe houses to help runaways escape from the South to the free states or Canada. This network came to be called the Underground Railroad. It was not a national organization but a makeshift group of committed individuals who did what they could to help runaway slaves find freedom. Since the whole point was to help slaves escape unnoticed, it is difficult to determine accurately how many people were involved. Some historians estimate that 75,000 slaves escaped with the help of about 3,000 black and white "conductors" in the fifty years before the Civil War.

The most famous conductor was Harriet Tubman. An escaped slave herself, she led more than three hundred slaves to freedom. Among the many other antislavery activists who risked their lives to help fugitive slaves were Levi Coffin in Ohio, Thomas Garrett in Delaware, and William Still in Pennsylvania. But most slaves running away to freedom had to make it on their own. No conductors, no safe houses, just their own courage and resourcefulness.

Harriet Tubman.

CHARLES PEYTON LUCAS

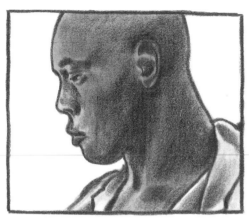

Charles Peyton Lucas.

"I started for the North with two companions; but it was cock-crowing before we reached the Potomac; so we went on a hill, and hid until the next (Sunday) night. Then we came back down, and tied our provisions into bundles on our backs, and started for the Potomac river—whether to wade it, swim it, or get drowned, we know not. We waded and swam, changing our ground as the water deepened. At last we reached the opposite bank in Maryland: we merely stopped to pour the water out of our boots, and then traveled on all wet, until morning; then we hid in the bushes. We traveled by night and concealed ourselves by day, for ten days and nights, suffering greatly from hunger and from rain, without shelter. One day in September, we sat on a mountain, exposed to a hot, broiling sun, and without food or drink. We could hear people at their work about us, but we did not dare ask for aid. For three days, we had neither food nor drink, excepting green corn. We sucked the juice for drink, and the corn itself was our only food. The effect of this was to weaken us very much.

"One night we came to a farmer's spring-house—I broke the lock and got a good pan of milk, but before I could find anything else, the dogs began to bark, so that we had to hurry off. We quaffed the milk with a good relish and it did us a deal of service. We drank at times muddy water from horse tracks: on one occasion, we were run very severely by dogs and men, but we got away from them. One morning between two and four o'clock, we came to a man tending a lime-kiln—he was asleep. We knew nothing of the way; so we concluded to awaken him, and ask the way, and if he tried to stop us, or have us caught, that we would kill him and throw him into the kiln. We awoke him and told him that our harvesting was done—we were hunting for work, as we had two days of work in. He did not believe it—said we were runaways. I took out my pistol, cocked and capped it, and the others produced, one a bayonet, and the other a bowie knife. The man approached us, saying still we were runaways. Had he offered to touch us we would have killed him, but

he proved to be the best friend we ever had. He told us our way, and regretted that he had no food. Said he, 'If you travel on, by day-light you will cross Mason and Dixon's line, and get among the Dutch. Keep away from the big road, walk near it, but not on it—walk in the daytime, but keep in the woods.' We followed his directions, and at ten o'clock next morning, we reached a Dutchman's house. The man was out—but the woman and girls set the table. We ate all they had in the house— I ate till I was ashamed. The good woman told us to avoid Shippenburg, as six had been carried back from there just before. She told us, if anybody questioned us, to say that we were going to Horse Shoe Bottom camp meeting on the Susquehanna. We did accordingly, and soon struck the track of the underground railroad, which we followed into the northern free States."

One of the most famous escapes from slavery was also one of the most imaginative. Henry "Box" Brown had himself nailed up in a wooden crate with only some water and some biscuits and arranged to be shipped from Richmond to Philadelphia.

White slaveowners feared runaways because they knew that news of successful escapes would spread the desire to run away like a contagious disease. A Louisiana doctor, Samuel Cartwright, published a ridiculous theory that blacks carried a particular disease he called "drapetomania—the disease causing Negroes to run away." His cure was to whip the desire to run out of the slave "suffering" from this nonexistent illness.

Henry "Box" Brown.

REBELLION!

The threat of violent slave rebellions frightened every slaveowner in history. Given Rome's history as a slave-supported empire, it is surprising that slave uprisings weren't a constant problem. Slave rebellions certainly occurred, but there was only one that threatened the stability of the empire. In 73 B.C. a Thracian gladiator named Spartacus, along with seventy others, escaped from the training school in Capua, pillaged the countryside, and recruited escaped slaves as he went. Roman troops sent to put down the revolt were repeatedly beaten and humiliated, which enhanced Spartacus's reputation among slaves and the poor across central Italy. Over the next two years, Spartacus's army of slaves and peasants grew to over 90,000 and was finally recognized in Rome as a serious threat. In the end, a Roman army led by Marcus Licinius Crassus crushed the revolt, killed Spartacus, and crucified 6,000 of his followers along the Via Appia, the main road leading to Rome. There was never a serious slave revolt in Rome again.

The Zanj revolts were the bloodiest slave rebellions in Islamic history. The Zanj were a Bantu-speaking people from East Africa who were taken as slaves in

opposite: Spartacus leads his slave army against the legions of Rome.

great numbers by the Abbasid Empire, which ruled what is now Iraq. The Zanj were at the very bottom of the social scale, even compared to other slaves. They were condemned to the hardest labor in the empire, the draining and cultivation of the broad salt flats of southern Iraq. They worked in large gangs of up to 5,000 men and were starved, beaten, and whipped without mercy. Malaria and a host of other diseases were rampant and only added to their misery. The continued brutality of their captors sparked a series of violent revolts, each put down with increasing ruthlessness. The last and most serious Zanj uprising began in A.D. 869. Ali b. Sahid al-Zanj (which means "master of the Zanj") led an army of slaves against the caliph (Arabic for "ruler"). Within two years the Zanj had captured a string of important port cities, including Basra, the largest port in Iraq. By 878 the Zanj had created their own state, and it posed a serious threat to the Abbassid caliphate. It took twelve years for the caliph to muster the forces necessary to push back the Zanj. Despite heroic efforts, the slaves were eventually overwhelmed by the Abbassid army. The Zanj capital city was taken in 883 after a three-year siege, and the leaders of the rebellion were executed. All told, between 100,000 and 300,000 slaves fought for their freedom against the most powerful empire in the Islamic world.

There were nearly sixty revolts aboard slave ships crossing the Atlantic recorded during the eighteenth and early nineteenth centuries.

MUTINY ON A SLAVE SHIP

In 1699 James Barbot described a slave uprising aboard his ship, the Albion-Frigate: *"One day, about one in the afternoon, after dinner, according to custom, we caused them, one by one, to go down between the decks, to have each his pint of water. Most of them were yet above deck and many of them were provided with knives which we had indiscreetly given them two or three days before, not suspecting the least attempt of this nature from them. It afterward appeared that others had pieces of iron which they had torn off the forecastle door, having premeditated this revolt. They had also broken off the shackles from the legs of several of their companions, which also served them. Thus armed they suddenly fell upon our men and stabbed one of the stoutest, who received fourteen or fifteen wounds from their knives so that he expired shortly. Next they assaulted our boatswain and cut off one of his legs so round the bone that he could not move, the nerves being cut through.*

"Others cut the cook's throat to the pipe and yet others wounded three of the sailors and threw one of them overboard from the forecastle, who, however, by good providence, got hold of the bowlin[e] of the foresail and saved himself, along the lower wale of the quarter-deck, where we stood in arms, firing on the revolted slaves, of whom we killed some and wounded many, which so terrified the rest that they gave way and dispersed themselves, some between decks and some under the fore-castle. Many of the most mutinous leaped overboard and drowned themselves with much resolution, showing no manner of concern for life.

"Thus we lost twenty-eight slaves and having mastered them, caused all to go betwixt decks, giving them good words. The next day, however, we had them all again upon deck and caused about thirty of the ringleaders to be severely whipt by all our men."

The crew of a slave ship desperately fight off escaped slaves armed with machetes.

Near the end of the eighteenth century, Haiti produced half of the world's coffee and sugar. There were 500,000 black slaves in Haiti and only 35,000 whites; there were also 35,000 free blacks and mulattos (people of mixed ancestry). When revolution exploded across France in 1789, Haitians expected the rights and liberties won by the revolutionaries to be granted to them since they were France's most profitable colony. When nothing changed, the slaves of Haiti took matters into their own hands. On August 14, 1791, the slaves broke out of their barracoons, torched every cane field, sugar mill, and planter's house, then attacked every white person they found. The machetes used to cut cane eighteen hours a day took only a split second to kill each white man, woman, and child who was caught. The free blacks and mulattos joined the spontaneous revolution. After the initial waves of chaos swept across the countryside, the revolution evolved into an organized attempt to overthrow the colonial government. A forty-five-year-old slave named François Dominique Toussaint L'Ouverture emerged as the revolution's leader.

FRANÇOIS DOMINIQUE TOUSSAINT L'OUVERTURE

François Dominique Toussant L'Ouverture.

François Dominique Toussaint L'Ouverture was one of the most important black leaders in the history of the Americas. He was the driving force in Haiti's struggle for independence and the first black national leader in the Western Hemisphere.

Born into slavery on the Breda sugar plantation outside Cap François, Haiti's busiest city, Toussaint de Breda (as he was known before the revolution) spent thirty years as a slave, working first as a coachman and then as the livestock steward, a job usually held by white men.

During the initial uprising, Toussaint served under the two leading slave generals, Jean-François and Biassou. In 1793 he became Biassou's chief lieutenant, and the slaves forced the French to abolish slavery in the colony. A year later Toussaint, now calling himself Toussaint L'Ouverture, was appointed commanding general of the colony's army. By 1796 he was the dominant political figure in Haiti. For the next five years he managed skillfully to wrest control of Haiti from the colonial authorities and repel attacks by both British and Spanish troops sent to take advantage of the island's unrest. Toussaint L'Ouverture was forced to take drastic action to hold the colony together, becoming, in effect, a dictator. But his leadership earned overwhelming support from the population, which was 90 percent ex-slave. He then set about to prove his administrative skills: He divided the country into six provinces, established a new court system, and overhauled the tax system. He established new schools and implemented a rebuilding program. In eighteen months he got two thirds of the plantations up and running again, an exceptional feat since almost every one of them had been burned to the ground. Toussaint L'Ouverture's rise to power coincided with the rise of the dictator Napoleon Bonaparte back in France. Bonaparte was determined to reestablish slavery in Haiti. Napoleon sent a great army to retake the island and force Toussaint L'Ouverture's resignation. Immediately after he submitted his resignation, Toussaint L'Ouverture was arrested and sent to France, where he was kept in prison until he died in April 1803. The French invasion and Toussaint L'Ouverture's arrest sparked bitter conflict between the French army and the Haitian revolutionaries. Over the next seven months 60,000 people died, either in battle or from an epidemic of yellow fever that swept across the island. Napoleon's troops suffered heavier losses than they had in any European campaign. They were forced to give up and evacuate the island by the end of the year. Finally, on January 1, 1804, L'Ouverture's successor, Dessalines, proclaimed Haiti's independence.

François Dominique Toussaint L'Ouverture left a legacy unmatched in the history of slavery. He led the only successful slave uprising in the Western Hemisphere, he forced France to abolish slavery in its most profitable colony, and he helped create the second independent nation in the Americas.

In the United States there was widespread fear among white Southerners that their slaves might someday rise up against them. But there were only three noteworthy slave uprisings in the pre–Civil War South, and two of those were broken up before they got started. There were so few slave rebellions in the South because the slaves knew without a doubt that any uprising would be brutally put down.

The most serious slave uprising in American history was led by Nat Turner. Turner was a carpenter in Southampton, Virginia, who said he was ordained by

God to carry out a great mission. His mission began on the night of Saturday, August 21, 1831, when Turner and six other slaves murdered his master, Joseph Travis, and his family, including a baby lying in its cradle. The group moved from house to house killing every white person they found. They gathered weapons and more followers as they went. Within forty-eight hours Turner and some sixty slaves butchered fifty-eight people, thirty-four of them children. Panic swept through the countryside and armed groups of whites rushed to confront the rebels. Most of the slaves were tracked down and killed within a week, but Turner and some of his men remained at large until the end of October. Within days of his capture Nat Turner was tried, convicted, and sentenced to death along with sixteen of his followers. He was hanged on November 11, 1831.

Nat Turner led the most serious slave uprising in American history.

ABOLITION:
AN END TO SLAVERY

Until the eighteenth century it was almost impossible to find anyone who spoke out against the inhumanity of slavery. The few individuals who saw that it was wrong to capture and sell human beings stood out because they were alone in their beliefs; slavery was accepted as a normal part of life nearly everywhere in the world. Organized opposition to slavery didn't begin until the early eighteenth century, and its impact varied greatly, depending on how important slavery was in different areas.

There were a few early opponents:

BARTOLOME DE LAS CASAS

Bartolome de Las Casas was twenty-four years old in 1498 when he accompanied his father on one of Columbus's expeditions to the West Indies. In 1510 he became the first priest ordained in the New World. At first he tried to profit from the enslavement of the Indians, but after witnessing the atrocities committed by Spanish troops, he had a change of heart and began to protest the treatment of the Indians by the

opposite: A slave family, set free after the Civil War, faces an uncertain future outside the plantation.

Bartolome de las Casas.

Spanish. He traveled back to Spain fourteen times to plead his case for an end to Indian slavery before the king of Spain, Charles V.

Las Casas's wishes came true: the enslavement of Indians did end, but not because of a worldwide attack of conscience. The Spanish, Portuguese, French, and English witnessed the Indians dying off in massive numbers, sometimes within days of their capture. It was apparent that the Indians were worthless as slave laborers and the Indian population was dropping so dramatically that they couldn't possibly meet the labor demands of the Europeans. Europe then focused on Africa as its new source of cheap labor. Las Casas himself owned African slaves until about 1544 but then came to believe that enslavement of anyone, Indian or African, was wrong. He wrote, "It is as unjust to enslave Negroes as Indians and for the same reasons." Las Casas died in 1566; his words wouldn't be published for three hundred years.

FATHER FERNANDO DE CONTRERAS

Another early hero in the battle against slavery was Father Fernando de Contreras, who risked his life to rescue hundreds of children from the worst pirates and slave traders on the Mediterranean Sea.

The most notorious pirates on the Barbary Coast of the Mediterranean were the Barbarossa brothers, Aruj and Khayr ad-Din. Born in Greece, the red-bearded brothers controlled a pirate fleet that captured tons of loot and enslaved hundreds of thousands of Christians. Khayr ad-Din once sent his master, the sultan of the Ottoman Empire, two hundred slave boys dressed in scarlet suits, each carrying a gold and a silver bowl. His daring and ambition, as well as his extravagant gifts, led Khayr ad-Din to a life among the elite of Islamic society that he enjoyed until his death.

Father Fernando de Contreras was a humble servant of God from Seville who operated several orphanages in Spain. He dedicated his life to the care and education of children. The enslavement of hundreds of children taken by the pirates of Barbary, however, moved him to take drastic action. He boldly traveled to Algiers to seek an audience with Khayr ad-Din, the most fearsome pirate in Islam. It was a long shot to be granted an audience with the pirate prince; Algiers was suffering a terrible drought, and it was doubtful he would be in any mood for the pleadings of a Spanish priest. In fact, Contreras feared he would be held for ransom himself. But, to the priest's surprise, he was allowed to see the pirate. Tales of Barbarossa's fearsome appearance and accounts of his many acts of savagery must have terrified Contreras. Barbarossa's face was framed by a thick red beard; it appeared as if dark red flames were leaping from his face. His eyes were intense, staring from beneath thick brows. The priest couldn't look into the pirate's eyes as he struggled to present his case for the children's release. On his long journey to Algiers he had considered many responses, but never did he expect the proposal Barbarossa laid before him. Father Contreras would be allowed to pray with the children, but their prayers should ask for rain, and if their prayers were answered, Barbarossa would allow the children to be ransomed. The priest was taken to the children, who were terrified but otherwise in good condition. They prayed together for three days with no results. Father Contreras feared Barbarossa was losing patience. As a last resort, he led the children in a procession through the streets of Algiers. Under the silent stares of the citizens, each child walked slowly, holding a lighted taper and reciting the litany in a trembling voice. Then it happened: The heavens burst forth with rain, drenching the children, the crowd, and one very thankful old priest. The rain didn't stop for three days, exactly the number of days they had spent in prayer.

Barbarossa seemed genuinely moved; he declared the priest a marabout, a powerful holy man. Father Contreras assured him that it was the work of God, not man. The pirate prince kept his word and allowed the priest to ransom the children (for

Father Contreras prays before Barbarossa.

3,000 ducats) and return with them to Spain. Fernando de Contreras returned to Algiers six more times in the years that followed to ransom more enslaved children. Each time Barbarossa took only the priest's wooden staff as collateral and each time Contreras sent the ransom money as promised.

A few individuals, such as Bartolome de Las Casas and Fernando de Contreras, couldn't hope to end slavery, but that didn't stop their courageous efforts. The recognition of slavery as an evil institution evolved gradually over time, but it wasn't until the late eighteenth century that organized groups made serious efforts to stop slavery.

The first abolitionists in America were a group of Quakers in Pennsylvania who published their objection to the slave trade in *The Germantown Protest* in 1688. The Quakers continued to speak out against slavery throughout the 1700s in the United States, particularly in Pennsylvania and Massachusetts. English Quakers were active, too. In 1783 they formed the first abolitionist organization, the Committee on the Slave Trade. The most influential English abolitionist of the eighteenth century was Granville Sharp. Sharp's passion for humanitarian causes led him to fight for the legal rights of slaves. His efforts that led to the groundbreaking ruling in the English courts that any slave who reached British soil would become legally free. This ruling made it clear that slavery could not exist under British law, and slavery was soon banned in England.

The leaders of the American Revolution struggled with the ethics of slavery, but many of them owned slaves. George Washington wrote in a letter in 1786, "I never mean (unless some peculiar circumstance compel me to do it) to possess another slave by purchase; it being among my first wishes to see some plan adopted, by which slavery in this country be abolished by slow, sure, and imperceptible degrees." Thomas Jefferson wrote, "The whole commerce between master and slave is a perpetual exercise of the most boisterous passions, the most unremitting despotism on the one part, and degrading submissions on the other. Our children see this, and learn to imitate it, and daily exercised in tyranny, cannot but be stamped by it with odious peculiarities." Yet these two men, founding fathers of our country, owed their livelihoods to slaves. Both their houses, Mount Vernon and Monticello, were built by slaves; slaves cooked and cleaned for them, and slaves worked their fields.

In 1776 there were roughly 2.5 million white Americans and 750,000 black Americans, and blacks and whites alike called for freedom. For black Americans, however, the call was not just for freedom from British rule but freedom from the tyranny of slavery. They took the phrase in the Declaration of Independence "All men are created equal" at face value. A petition received by the legislature of Massachusetts in 1777, written by a group of black Americans, said, "Prosper in your present glorious struggle for liberty." They then asked the lawmakers to remember that they "have in common with all other men a natural and inalienable right to that freedom which the Great Parent of the universe hath bestowed equally on all mankind and which they have never forfeited by any compact or agreement whatever."

Black Americans were a part of the Revolutionary War from the very beginning. The Boston Massacre in 1770 was one of the pivotal events that led to war with the British. One of the first Americans shot down by the British troops was Crispus Attucks, a former slave. When the war began, the Revolutionary Army refused blacks. But the British Army promised freedom to any slave who fought on their side. Faced with the mass defection of thousands of potential soldiers, the Revolutionary Army leaders quickly changed their minds. In 1775 George Washington's army had 5,000 black soldiers, both slave and free, and blacks fought at the battle of Lexington and Concord. Georgia and South Carolina, the two southernmost colonies, refused to enlist black soldiers and lost 25,000 slaves to the British side. When the Americans won the war, those slaves who expected to be freed were bitterly disappointed. The infant nation was already split in its attitude toward slavery. In order to keep the nation together, the Continental Congress, charged with writing a constitution in 1787, was forced to compromise. States were given the freedom to decide individually whether to allow slavery. The purchase of slaves brought directly from Africa would become illegal in twenty years (1807), and for the purpose of political representation, slaves would count as three-fifths of a person.

Free blacks had been active in the antislavery movement since the Revolutionary War. With few resources and no political power it was difficult for them to be heard, but they persevered. Some, such as Henry Highland Garnet, demanded the immediate and violent destruction of American slavery. He openly encouraged slaves to kill their masters. Others, like Frederick Douglass and Sojourner Truth, sought a peaceful path to freedom.

FREDERICK DOUGLASS

Frederick Douglass was the most influential former slave abolitionist in the United States. Born a slave in Maryland around 1817, he escaped his bondage in 1838 to become an author, newspaper publisher, and popular abolitionist lecturer.

As Frederick Bailey, he worked as a field hand, then as a caulker in the boatyards, until he borrowed the travel papers of a free black sailor and escaped to Massachusetts. There he changed his name, got married, and joined the abolitionist movement.

He was always a controversial figure, often arguing with his fellow abolitionists—he fought with William Lloyd Garrison, white publisher of antislavery literature, over politics, and with Sojourner Truth, militant feminist and abolitionist ex-slave, over religion. Many white men were angered by his words or perhaps threatened by his obvious intelligence and skill as a writer and speaker. Some accused him of making

Frederick Douglass.

up his past as a slave. To silence his critics he wrote his autobiography, Narrative of the Life of Frederick Douglass, an American Slave: Written by Himself, *in 1845.*

He traveled to England and became hugely popular there. English supporters arranged to buy his freedom so Douglass could return home to continue his work to end slavery. In his newspaper, first called the North Star, *then simply* Frederick Douglass' Paper, *he not only condemned the slave trade but also attacked the segregation of public schools and churches and challenged the Christianity of slaveowners. He also advocated equal rights for women. His dedication and outspokenness earned him passionate followers and bitter enemies.*

After the passage of the Fugitive Slave Act in 1850, Douglass became convinced that civil war was the only answer to the slavery issue. To Douglass, the political causes of the war were insignificant. In 1864 he wrote, "No war, but an abolition war; no peace but an abolition peace; liberty for all, chains for none; the black man a soldier in war, a laborer in peace; a voter at the South as well as the North; America his permanent home, and all Americans his fellow-countrymen."

After the Civil War and emancipation, Douglass continued his work, recognizing the need for drastic social reforms. In an 1869 essay entitled "We Are Not Yet Quite Free" he wrote, "We have been turned out of the house of bondage, but we have not yet been fully admitted to the glorious temple of American liberty." Knowing that the road to racial equality was long, he concluded, "The future is clouded with doubt and danger."

Frederick Douglass spent his life working for justice and equality for all Americans. The ex-slave, teacher, lecturer, publisher, and diplomat died in 1895. In his autobiography he eloquently summed up his life: "I have lived several lives in one. First, the life of slavery; secondly, the life of a fugitive from slavery; thirdly, the life of comparative freedom; fourthly, the life of conflict and battle; and fifthly, the life of victory, if not complete, at least assured. To those who have suffered in slavery, I can say I too have suffered. To those who have taken some risks and encountered hardships in the flight from bondage, I can say I too have endured and risked. To those who have battled for liberty, brotherhood, and citizenship, I can say I too have battled; and to those who have lived to enjoy the fruits of victory, I can say I too live and rejoice."

White abolitionists worked with black activists to spread their antislavery message. William Lloyd Garrison started his antislavery newspaper *The Liberator* in 1831. In it he spoke for the immediate elimination of slavery and demanded that women be granted the right to vote. He encouraged the Northern states to secede from the Union, whose constitution, he believed, protected slavery.

John Brown, another white abolitionist, fought slavery with violence. Brown had fought in bloody battles in Kansas as it was deciding whether to enter the Union as a free or a slave state. He came east in 1859 with a bold plan to seize the federal arsenal in Harpers Ferry, Virginia (now West Virginia), and use the weapons to liberate the slaves. He sought support from abolitionist leaders, including Frederick Douglass. Douglass recognized Brown's courage and devotion but saw little chance for his plan to succeed, so he tried to discourage him. Douglass was not successful. Brown, with twenty-one supporters, attacked the arsenal on the evening of October 16, 1859. In less than thirty-six hours the raid was over, a complete failure. Federal troops quickly killed most of his group and captured Brown. He was tried for treason and hanged. His rebellion failed, but he became a hero to black Americans, a martyr to the abolitionists, and a demon to the supporters of slavery. The jury is still out on John Brown's historical significance, but his actions convinced many on both sides that the issue of slavery would only be settled by war. On the way to the gallows Brown handed his jailer a piece of paper on which he had written, "I, John Brown, am now quite certain

John Brown believed in abolition at any cost.

that the crimes of this guilty land will never be purged away but with blood." He was right.

In the nineteenth century, the institution of slavery was changing around the world. In some places it disappeared completely; in others it became as prevalent as it had been in the ancient world. By the 1840s the transatlantic trade in human beings was legally dead, but all the European powers allowed the ownership of slaves to continue in their colonies, where enormous amounts of money were generated by slave labor. Since the economic might of these colonies was dependent on a steady supply of new slaves, the trade continued whether it was legal or not. Slave smugglers did big business. The British navy tried in vain to stop the illegal trade. American shipbuilders from New York to New Orleans were building fast ships that could outrun the Royal navy just for the slave trade. British merchant ships ignored their own government's laws, as did ships from practically every country. The potential profits were just too large to pass up. In the 1840s, a slave ship captain could get a cargo of slaves from an African dealer for about $10 a head and sell them in Cuba for more than $600 a head. At the same time, the U.S. government looked the other way as slave ships landed in South Carolina, Georgia, and Louisiana. Not one slave smuggler was charged or tried until 1862, when the Erie was captured off the African coast with 182 men, 106 women, and 612 children on board. The slaves were taken to Liberia, on the African coast, and set free. The captain of the *Erie,* Nathaniel Gordon, was tried, convicted, and hanged. The slave trade to America died with him. Large-scale, government-supported slavery in the New World was extinct when Brazil finally abolished slavery in 1888.

THE CIVIL WAR ENDS AMERICAN SLAVERY

By the 1860s America was bitterly divided between the free states in the North and the slave states in the South. At the time there was a lot of talk about other issues that were also leading to war. Many Northerners thought the war was necessary to preserve the Union; to Southerners the war was needed to preserve each state's right of self-determination. But it soon became clear that the battle was really over the future of slavery in America. President Lincoln issued the Emancipation Proclamation on January 1, 1863. It declared all slaves free, but it could have no effect on the 4 million slaves in the South unless the Union army won the war and liberated them. The war raged on for four years, until the Confederate forces under General Robert E. Lee surrendered to the Union army's General Ulysses S. Grant on April 9, 1865 at Appomattox Courthouse, Virginia. It was and still is the bloodiest conflict in American history. More than 400,000 soldiers died. More than a million were wounded. Nearly 250,000 black Americans fought in the war and 38,000 died. As the long and painful process of rebuilding and reuniting the country began, Congress formally ended slavery in the United States. The Thirteenth Amendment abolished slavery, the Fourteenth Amendment granted black Americans equal rights as citizens, and the Fifteenth Amendment gave them the right to vote. Slavery was gone, but it left deep divisions in the country that have yet to completely heal.

Confederate troops surprise a pair of Union soldiers.

SLAVERY TODAY

The plantations are gone and the horrors of the Middle Passage are distant history, but slavery is with us today and has had a significant presence in our modern world. The great events of the twentieth century dramatically changed our world and also changed the face of slavery. For millennia slavery had been primarily an economic institution. Slave labor generated wealth for slaveowners. Simply owning slaves was a statement of economic status. The trade in slaves was so attractive because there was a lot of money to be made in it. In the twentieth century, however, slave labor was often part of a political policy rather than an economic one. Totalitarian governments (those that control every part of their people's lives) used the threat of forced labor to maintain control over their subjects, or slavery was used to punish enemies of the state. In its most drastic form, slavery was used as a means of slowly killing off unwanted groups of people. Slavery's economic benefits became secondary.

Forced labor differs from the classic definition of slavery in that its victims are not usually bought and sold as property but are taken at gunpoint and set to work

opposite: A young boy labors in a textile processing plant in Bangladesh.

Two women watch as their fellow inmates walk through the snow to work at a Siberian labor camp.

for the benefit of the government. Forced labor had long been part of Russian history, but after the Russian Revolution in 1917, it became official state policy. The Communist Party of the new Soviet Union pronounced that their new government would free the workers from economic exploitation, but according to Soviet law all citizens were subject to compulsory labor. Under Joseph Stalin, Soviet dictator from 1927 until his death in 1953, tens of millions of his own people were shipped off to slave labor camps in the most desolate parts of the country. Anyone who voiced any opposition to Stalin or his government was arrested and sent away without trial. Families might never know what happened to their loved ones; they were simply taken away by the secret police. In 1947, at the height of Stalin's reign of terror, there were an estimated 10 to 12 million slave laborers in Soviet-controlled Europe and Asia. Most were in camps in Siberia and central Asia; some of the camps were north of the Arctic Circle. Conditions were miserable no matter where they were.

The laborers were forced to work for food. Better workers got better food; those who didn't work hard enough to satisfy the guards starved to death or froze in the Arctic cold. In some camps the death rate was over 30 percent.

ALEXANDER ROLIN

Alexander Rolin described his experience as a slave laborer in the gulag in the Kolyma River region, one of the coldest and most desolate places on earth.

"I, Alexander Rolin, am a former officer of the Red Army, of peasant origin. . . . I was arrested on July 2, 1938, as a member of a counter-revolutionary, diversionist-wrecking, military-terrorist organization . . .

"In reality, I never and nowhere belonged to any conspiratorial group; there was merely a campaign being waged for the consolidation of Stalin's regime, a campaign directed against the highest army commanders, party and administrative officials, who remembered better times and a more authoritative leadership and by their presence somewhat weakened the complete authority of the leader.

"My case dragged on, and the peak of the wave of arrests was passing, and in the end, the Revolutionary Tribunal in closed session sentenced me to six years of forced labor.

"I served my forced labor sentence in a local colony of the NKVD [Stalin's Internal Affairs Commission], in Kolyma, and in Nikolayevsk-on-the-Amur. At that time there were 500 prisoners in the local colony of the NKVD, 800,000 prisoners in Kolyma and 10,000 prisoners in Nikolayevsk-on-the-Amur.

"The working day, including the time required to go to and from work, totaled 12 hours. Work was done during any weather, and this considerably increased the death rate among the prisoners in the North.

"Food. *For those fulfilling their norm, 600 grams of bread, once soup and once groats; for those overfilling their norm, 800 grams of bread, and twice soup and once groats; for those underfilling their norm, 200 grams of bread, once soup, and grits. Once or twice a week, salted fish; and once or twice a month, meat dishes.*

"Housing conditions. *Long, poorly built barracks, with one or two iron stoves*

Alexander Rolin.

(only around the stoves was warm), with long double-decker cots and a sack filled with straw or sawdust for the prisoner. Congestion, filth, vermin. Once or twice a month, a change of poorly washed clothes.

"Winter clothing. *Old and worn and dirty cotton mackinaw, cotton trousers, and work shoes. All these conditions create a situation in which the weak are doomed to die and the strong are destined to wither slowly.*

"*In my days, the Kolyma camp was distinguished for an especially atrocious regime. There all prisoners who could not fill their norms for some reason (old age, weakness, lack of training in physical labor) were turned over to special detachments of three so-called troikas [groups of three men appointed by the camp commander to act as judge, jury, and executioners] who, as a rule, sentenced them to be shot, and carried out the sentence, for alleged sabotage, or else lengthened their sentence.*

"*Colonel of the NKVD Garanin was particularly known for his cruelty. He personally and arbitrarily shot prisoners who were not at work for some reason during his visit to a given camp.*

"*The result: yearly 100,000 prisoners were sent to Kolyma, and only about 10,000 returned.*

"*During my stay, the majority of prisoners were workers or peasants. I met among them persons who had been confined for five or six years and still did not know the reason for their arrest and the length of their sentence.*

"*I worked in the camp for about three years, was then released, and directly sent to the front, was surrounded and taken prisoner, and, despite the fact that I never in my life committed any crime against either my country or my people, I cannot return home, as I would be liquidated as an enemy of Stalin.*

"*January 26, 1949*   *ALEXANDER ROLIN*"

Stalin's successor, Nikita Krushchev, granted amnesty to many political prisoners, and the numbers of people in forced labor camps dropped to under a million by 1957, at least according to some sources. But until the fall of the Communist system in 1989, slave labor camps continued to be part of Russian life.

The Nazi Party took control of Germany in 1933 and immediately began building the foundation for a massive slave labor system. Concentration camps were built throughout Germany. These weren't part of the ordinary prison system; they were used to detain political prisoners, meaning anyone perceived as an enemy of the "new" Germany. From the very beginning prisoners were forced into heavy labor with no compensation; in other words, they were slaves. By 1938 the Nazis realized that the rapidly growing numbers of concentration camp inmates could be used as cheap labor for German industry. Germany had conquered most of Europe by the end of 1942 and expanded the camps into the conquered territories. These camps were operated by the SS—the military arm of the Nazi Party—and their reputation for cruelty and mass murder was made in these camps. Most of the camps outside of Germany were in Poland, including the infamous Auschwitz-Birkenau, which was by far the largest. German industrial corporations eagerly accepted the opportunity to exploit the large pool of slave laborers and built factories close to each camp. The biggest names in German industry—BMW, Daimler-Benz, I. G. Farben, Krupp, and a long list of others—used the slaves of the Nazis as laborers.

Slave laborers march outside the gates of Auschwitz-Birkenau, the Nazi death camp.

Roughly 7.5 million civilians (taken from conquered territories throughout Europe) and 2 million prisoners of war were forced to work in German camps and factories. Almost all were treated badly. Starvation, overwork, torture, and murder on an unprecedented scale were carried out with brutal efficiency. Treatment of prisoners varied according to the Nazi concept of racial superiority. Those who shared the ideal racial characteristics of the Nazis—that is, the physical traits of white, northern Europeans—usually received adequate food, water, and shelter. Southern Europeans were considered inferior by the Nazis, and they received harsher treatment. The Slavic peoples of Eastern Europe and Russia were way down on the list, and they bore the brunt of Nazi brutality. Starvation, overwork, and summary execution were everyday occurrences. "Slavs are slaves" read signs outside Krupp weapons plants. Jews, according to the twisted Nazi ideology, were not even human beings; they were subhuman and had to be exterminated. If they weren't murdered as soon as they arrived at the camps, they were put to work and fed just enough to keep them alive until a new shipment of slaves arrived. In 1942 Alfried Krupp wrote a letter to Hitler endorsing his plan to eliminate Jews, Gypsies, criminals, and anti-Nazi Germans. He proposed a policy of "extermination through work" in which Germany, and of course Krupp and his business interests, would benefit from the labors of these slaves before they were starved and worked to death.

After the Nazis were defeated in the spring of 1945, the rest of the world got to see the horrors of the Nazi slave labor system. In just over ten years Hitler had created the biggest and most brutal system of slavery in history.

Drastic attempts to reorganize a society by using mass murder and forced labor did not end with Hitler and the Nazis. In 1975 the Communist Khmer Rouge movement, led by Pol Pot, overthrew the government of Cambodia. Pol Pot immediately ordered the execution of all the doctors, teachers, engineers—even anyone who wore eyeglasses—in an attempt to rid the country of any educated people who might challenge the Khmer Rouge's plans to create an agricultural society supported by the hard work of all Cambodians. In other words, everyone in the entire country would be reduced to slave laborers. Millions were sent into the countryside to work. Whole cities were evacuated. It is estimated that at least one million Cambodians died before Pol Pot's government was overthrown by Vietnamese forces in January of 1979. Pol Pot and his supporters retreated to the hills bordering Thailand, where he died in hiding in 1998.

Slavery still exists around the world. Anti-Slavery International, which works to eliminate all forms of servitude, issues quarterly reports on the modern versions of slavery it finds around the world. It works with other organizations to provide research information to individual governments and international organizations, such as the United Nations. Anti-Slavery International and other human rights groups have found chattel slavery—defined as the sale and ownership of one person by another—in Sudan and Mauritania. In 1995 investigators witnessed slaves sold in markets in northern Sudan. The victims were Christian or animist Africans (animists believe in the spiritual forces of nature) from the southern part of the country who were abducted by Arab militias. The witnesses reported inhumane and degrading treatment that is tolerated and even endorsed by Sudan's Arab government.

The enslavement of children remains all too common throughout Asia. Between 500,000 and 1 million children are forcibly employed in the production of handmade carpets in Pakistan. Many more thousands are exploited in the carpet industries in India and Nepal. These children work at their looms in dingy shops weaving the intricate patterns so desired in international markets. They are forced to work from before dawn until late at night and are paid only pennies a day. Many are trapped in a system that takes their pitiful wages to pay off loans taken out by their families. Others are kidnapped and made to work until they pay off the ransom set by their abductors. Yet others are given away to labor contractors who promise the child's family that he or she will be educated and taught a trade; these children end up working at a loom for little money and have no future.

IQBAL MASIH

Iqbal Masih.

Iqbal Masih was sold to a carpetmaker by his parents when he was only four years old. For the next six years he was chained to his loom, weaving carpets fourteen hours a day, six days a week. Iqbal refused to accept his fate, he often defied his master and refused to work, in spite of the severe beating he got each time he did so. He tried to escape many times and only got more beatings for his trouble. Finally, when he was ten, Iqbal slipped out of his chains and made it to freedom. With the help of the Bonded Labor Liberation Front, a Pakistani human rights organization, Iqbal became a powerful spokesman for the freedom of child laborers throughout Pakistan and the world. He assisted in the liberation of 3,000 children and was honored for his work by the International Labor Organization and by Reebok, who awarded him its Human Rights Youth in Action Award. This small, courageous boy was seen around the world as a leader in the fight against the enslavement of children. Those who ran the carpet industry in Pakistan had a different opinion of the boy. They attacked his work in the media, attempting to discredit him, and occasionally threatened him with violence. He told his friends and supporters that the threats only made him work harder. Iqbal Masih was shot dead on April 16, 1995. Eight hundred mourners were at the Muridke cemetery for his funeral. The next week 3,000 demonstrators, at least half of them under twelve years old, marched through the streets demanding an end to child labor. Iqbal's murder remains unsolved, but few doubt the involvement of the carpet industry.

In Southeast Asia children are forced into the sex industry. Child prostitution is a big business throughout the region, but it is centered in Bangkok, Thailand. Hundreds of thousands of boys and girls, some as young as eight years old, are available to customers for sex. Many of these children, like the carpet slaves of Pakistan, are sold into slavery by their desperately poor families. Some are abducted, driven to a city far away, and put to work. In Bangkok's red-light district, where this terrible trade flourishes, child prostitutes are said to be in their prime when they are ten, by twenty they are too old, and by thirty they are dead.

In the not-so-distant past slavery was universal, accepted as a part of life in every culture; today it exists in far fewer places, but it still exists. Mankind has come a long way in understanding that every human being has a right to be free, but those still being kept against their will deserve the same freedom that the rest of us take for granted. Perhaps in the near future every nation on the planet will recognize and restore the fundamental human rights of all people. Only then can the final chapter in the long history of slavery be written.

GLOSSARY

agora the open area in the center of most Greek cities where trading and business took place.

atriensis the person (usually a slave) in charge of the everyday operation of a wealthy Roman household.

barracoon a building in which captured slaves were held.

bugu a debt slave during the Ming dynasty in ancient China.

chikote a type of whip used in the East African slave trade, usually made from a thin strip of animal hide.

coartacion the policy of the colonial government of Cuba that allowed slaves to buy their freedom.

coffle a line of slaves roped or chained together.

cowrie shells brightly colored seashells found primarily in the Indian Ocean and used as currency in some parts of Africa.

decuria a group of ten Roman slaves responsible for a specific task.

denarii a unit of Roman currency.

dentalia seashells found on the west coast of Vancouver Island in Canada and once used by Native Americans along the Pacific Coast as money.

dhow an Arab sailing ship with a large triangular sail.

dispesator a Roman slave in charge of the household supplies.

factor the person in charge of a slave-trading operation.

familia urbana the staff of slaves in a wealthy Roman household.

gulag a forced labor camp in the Soviet Union.

janissary a slave soldier of the Ottoman Empire.

mamluk a slave soldier in Egypt during the Middle Ages. A Mamluk dynasty ruled Egypt from 1250 to 1517.

manumission granting a slave his or her freedom.

metics resident foreigners in ancient Greece.

plebeian a free commoner of ancient Rome.

potlatch a great feast among the Native American peoples in the Pacific Northwest.

procurator a person (often a slave) responsible for all purchasing and business outside a Roman household.

quaestor the paymaster of a Roman army, often responsible for organizing the sale of captured enemy soldiers.

quilombo a colony of runaway slaves in Brazil.

serf a peasant in medieval Europe who was forced to live and work on land owned by a lord.

shekel a unit of currency in ancient Mesopotamia.

sileniarius the person (usually a slave) responsible for the security of a wealthy Roman household.

slave factory a holding facility for captured slaves that often included many buildings, such as barracks for guards and staff, warehouses for trade goods, and repair shops, as well as the buildings that confined the slaves.

tlacotin an Aztec slave.

A TIMELINE OF SLAVERY

C. 4000 B.C. First civilizations appear in Mesopotamia. Slaves are used for construction, farming, and domestic service.

C. 3000 B.C. Egyptian pharaohs use peasant farmers to build massive pyramids and temples. Slavery is common in Egypt but not critical to Egyptian civilization.

C. 400 B.C. Golden Age of ancient Greece. Slaves outnumber free citizens in Athens.

73 B.C. A Thracian gladiator named Spartacus leads an uprising of 70,000 slaves, the largest slave revolt in Roman history.

C. A.D. 200 The Roman Empire is at the height of its power and is dependent on slave labor.

c. A.D. 600 Rapid spread of Islam begins. International trade in slaves crosses Africa and the Middle East.

A.D. 869–883 Between 100,000 and 300,000 slaves called the Zanj, taken from Africa, revolt against the Abbassid caliph in southern Iraq.

c. 1000–1400 Great African kingdoms of Ghana and Mali rule western Africa.

1250–1517 Mamluks, the slave soldiers of Egypt, take control of the country and import millions of slaves. Many are used to fill their armies.

1266 Italian merchants establish a trading colony at Kaffa, a port on the Crimean Peninsula on the Black Sea. It becomes the largest market for slaves in the Middle Ages.

1300 The Ottoman Empire is born. It becomes the largest slave-dependent society since Rome.

1481 The Portuguese build the first slave factory at Elmina on the west coast of Africa.

1492 Columbus lands in the New World. He enslaves 500 Taino Indians and takes them back to Spain.

1540 The Portuguese introduce sugar cane to Brazil, which sparks the massive importation of African slaves to work the sugar plantations.

1540–1870 Eleven million African slaves are shipped to the Americas.

1783 The first abolitionist organization, the Committee on the Slave Trade, is formed by English Quakers.

1791 Haitian slaves sucessfully revolt against their French colonial rulers. François Dominique Toussaint L'Ouverture becomes the first black national leader in the Western Hemisphere.

1793 Eli Whitney invents the cotton gin. Cotton production explodes, as does the demand for African slaves to work the cotton fields.

1831 Nat Turner leads a bloody slave uprising in Virginia. Fifty-eight whites are killed. Turner is captured and executed.

1859 John Brown leads a failed attack on the federal arsenal in Harpers Ferry, Virginia (now West Virginia), hoping to spark a national slave revolt.

1863 Abraham Lincoln issues the Emancipation Proclamation, which declares all slaves free.

1864 The Civil War ends when Confederate forces surrender at Appomattox Courthouse, Virginia. Slavery is over in the United States.

1888 Brazil becomes the last country in the Western Hemisphere to abolish slavery.

1927–53 Tens of millions are sent to slave labor camps in the Soviet Union during the dictatorship of Joseph Stalin.

1933–45 The Nazi Party in Germany operates slave labor camps across Europe. 10 million people are forced into slavery. More than 6 million are killed (mostly Jews and Eastern Europeans).

1975–79 The Khmer Rouge Communist regime in Cambodia sends millions to agricultural labor camps. Over 1 million die.

Today Illegal slavery persists in Brazil, Pakistan, Thailand, Mauritania, Sudan, and other places around the world.

BIBLIOGRAPHY

Davidson, Basil. *The African Slave Trade*. Boston: Little, Brown, 1961.

Dow, George Francis. *Slave Ships and Slaving*. Salem, Mass.: Marine Research Society, 1927.

Jewitt, John Rodgers. *The Adventures and Sufferings of John R. Jewitt: Captive of Maquinna*. Seattle: University of Washington Press, 1987.

Lewis, Bernard. *Race and Slavery in the Middle East*. Oxford: Oxford University Press, 1990.

Meltzer, Milton. *Slavery: A World History*. New York: Da Capo, 1993.

Phillips, William D. *Slavery from Roman Times to the Early Transatlantic Trade*. Minneapolis: University of Minnesota Press, 1985.

Rodriguez, Junius P., gen. ed. *The Historical Encyclopedia of World Slavery*. Santa Barbara, Calif.: ABC–CLIO, 1997.

Thomas, Hugh. *The Slave Trade: The Story of the Atlantic Slave Trade, 1440–1870*. New York: Simon and Schuster, 1997.

INDEX